ALABASTER

ALABASTER

Contact
hello@alabasterco.com
www.alabasterco.com

Alabaster Co. The Bible Beautiful.
Visual imagery & thoughtful design integrated within the Bible.
Cultivating conversation between art, beauty, & faith.

Founded in 2016.

NLT.

ARTIST INTRODUCTION

——

Genesis is an ancient book of poetry and prose, recording and reflecting the earliest encounters between God and humankind.

It is the story of a burgeoning world just beginning and a story of humans learning how to live in the light of a covenant-making God. The characters of Genesis consistently find themselves walking towards uncertain futures. But—equipped with the promises of God—they press forward, learning to trust God in spite of their mistakes and failures. As we read and study Genesis, we unearth truths that form, shape, and guide us, even today.

In making this book, we used the colors brown and orange to guide our creative direction. Brown, first to harken back to Genesis 2:7—*Then the Lord God formed the man from the dust of the ground. He breathed the breath of life into the man's nostrils, and the man became a living person*. But, also, to represent the figurative "dirt" in the book—the angered, grieved, and sad stories that occur within Genesis. Orange is used to symbolize the opposite; it represents the stories of redemption in Genesis and a God who is creative, compassionate, and promise-making. Our images focus on landscapes, people, and objects to show the beautiful and diverse world God has made around us.

Ultimately, Genesis shows us that being human is messy. There are moments of strained relationships, violence, distrust, and fear. But through it, the text teaches us what it looks like to persevere and find hope in God. Though following God might not always look like what we expect, His promises protect and sustain us. As we read this text, may it transform not only our personal lives but also the world around us. Amen.

BOOK OF

GENESIS

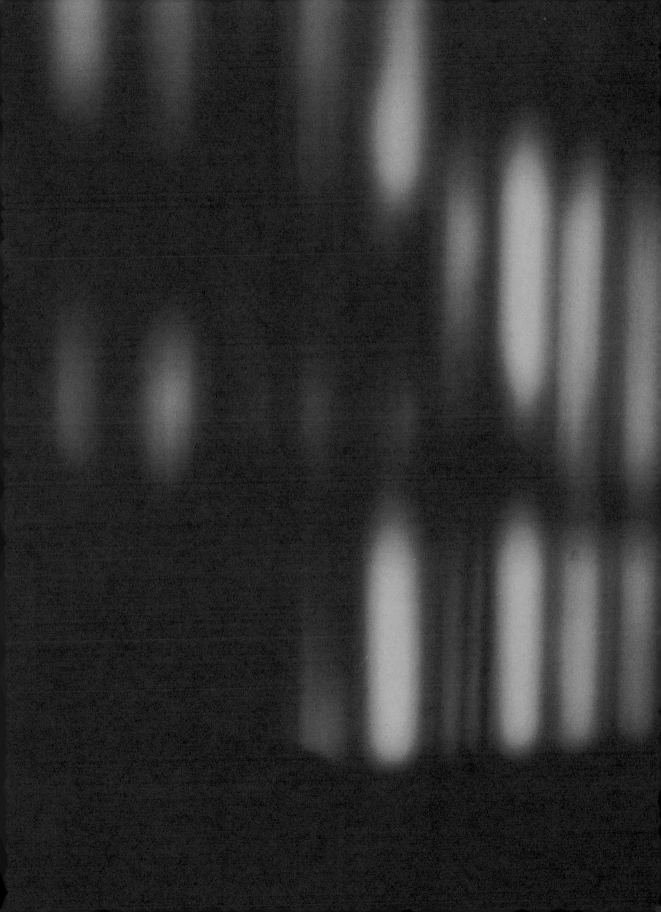

1

THE ACCOUNT OF CREATION

[1] In the beginning God created the heavens and the earth. [2] The earth was formless and empty, and darkness covered the deep waters. And the Spirit of God was hovering over the surface of the waters. [3] Then God said, "Let there be light," and there was light. [4] And God saw that the light was good. Then he separated the light from the darkness. [5] God called the light "day" and the darkness "night." And evening passed and morning came, marking the first day. [6] Then God said, "Let there be a space between the waters, to separate the waters of the heavens from the waters of the earth." [7] And that is what happened. God made this space to separate the waters of the earth from the waters of the heavens. [8] God called the space "sky." And evening passed and morning came, marking the second day. [9] Then God said, "Let the waters beneath the sky flow together into one place, so dry ground may appear." And that is what happened. [10] God called the dry ground "land" and the waters "seas." And God saw that it was good. [11] Then God said, "Let the land sprout with vegetation—every sort of seed-bearing plant, and trees that grow seed-bearing fruit. These seeds will then produce the kinds of plants and trees from which they came." And that is what happened. [12] The land produced vegetation—all sorts of seed-bearing plants, and trees with seed-bearing fruit. Their seeds produced plants and trees of the same kind. And God saw that it was good. [13] And evening passed and morning came, marking the third day. [14] Then God said, "Let lights appear in the sky to separate the day from the night. Let them be signs to mark the seasons, days, and years. [15] Let these lights in the sky shine down on the earth." And that is what happened. [16] God made two great lights—the larger one to govern the day, and the smaller one to govern the night. He also made the stars. [17] God set these lights in the sky to light the earth, [18] to govern the day and night, and

to separate the light from the darkness. And God saw that it was good. [19] And evening passed and morning came, marking the fourth day. [20] Then God said, "Let the waters swarm with fish and other life. Let the skies be filled with birds of every kind." [21] So God created great sea creatures and every living thing that scurries and swarms in the water, and every sort of bird—each producing offspring of the same kind. And God saw that it was good. [22] Then God blessed them, saying, "Be fruitful and multiply. Let the fish fill the seas, and let the birds multiply on the earth." [23] And evening passed and morning came, marking the fifth day. [24] Then God said, "Let the earth produce every sort of animal, each producing offspring of the same kind—livestock, small animals that scurry along the ground, and wild animals." And that is what happened. [25] God made all sorts of wild animals, livestock, and small animals, each able to produce offspring of the same kind. And God saw that it was good. [26] Then God said, "Let us make human beings in our image, to be like us. They will reign over the fish in the sea, the birds in the sky, the livestock, all the wild animals on the earth, and the small animals that scurry along the ground." [27] So God created human beings in his own image. In the image of God he created them; male and female he created them. [28] Then God blessed them and said, "Be fruitful and multiply. Fill the earth and govern it. Reign over the fish in the sea, the birds in the sky, and all the animals that scurry along the ground." [29] Then God said, "Look! I have given you every seed-bearing plant throughout the earth and all the fruit trees for your food. [30] And I have given every green plant as food for all the wild animals, the birds in the sky, and the small animals that scurry along the ground—everything that has life." And that is what happened. [31] Then God looked over all he had made, and he saw that it was very good! And evening passed and morning came, marking the sixth day.

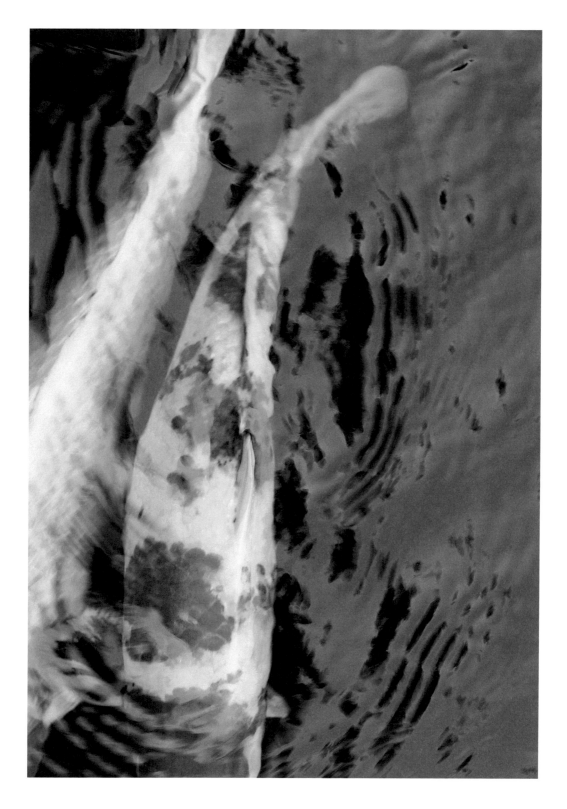

2

¹ So the creation of the heavens and the earth and everything in them was completed. ² On the seventh day God had finished his work of creation, so he rested from all his work. ³ And God blessed the seventh day and declared it holy, because it was the day when he rested from all his work of creation. ⁴ This is the account of the creation of the heavens and the earth.

THE MAN AND WOMAN IN EDEN

When the Lord God made the earth and the heavens, [5] neither wild plants nor grains were growing on the earth. For the Lord God had not yet sent rain to water the earth, and there were no people to cultivate the soil. [6] Instead, springs came up from the ground and watered all the land. [7] Then the Lord God formed the man from the dust of the ground. He breathed the breath of life into the man's nostrils, and the man became a living person. [8] Then the Lord God planted a garden in Eden in the east, and there he placed the man he had made. [9] The Lord God made all sorts of trees grow up from the ground—trees that were beautiful and that produced delicious fruit. In the middle of the garden he placed the tree of life and the tree of the knowledge of good and evil. [10] A river flowed from the land of Eden, watering the garden and then dividing into four branches. [11] The first branch, called the Pishon, flowed around the entire land of Havilah, where gold is found. [12] The gold of that land is exceptionally pure; aromatic resin and onyx stone are also found there. [13] The second branch, called the Gihon, flowed around the entire land of Cush. [14] The third branch, called the Tigris, flowed east of the land of Asshur. The fourth branch is called the Euphrates. [15] The Lord God placed the man in the Garden of Eden to tend and watch over it. [16] But the Lord God warned him, "You may freely eat the fruit of every tree in the garden— [17] except the tree of the knowledge of good and evil. If you eat its fruit, you are sure to die."

¹⁸ Then the Lord God said "It is not good for the man to be alone. I will make a helper who is just right for him." ¹⁹ So the Lord God formed from the ground all the wild animals and all the birds of the sky. He brought them to the man to see what he would call them, and the man chose a name for each one. ²⁰ He gave names to all the livestock, all the birds of the sky, and all the wild animals. But still there was no helper just right for him. ²¹ So the Lord God caused the man to fall into a deep sleep. While the man slept, the Lord God took out one of the man's ribs and closed up the opening. ²² Then the Lord God made a woman from the rib, and he brought her to the man. ²³ "At last!" the man exclaimed. "This one is bone from my bone, and flesh from my flesh! She will be called 'woman,' because she was taken from 'man.'" ²⁴ This explains why a man leaves his father and mother and is joined to his wife, and the two are united into one. ²⁵ Now the man and his wife were both naked, but they felt no shame.

3

THE MAN AND WOMAN SIN

¹ The serpent was the shrewdest of all the wild animals the Lord God had made. One day he asked the woman, "Did God really say you must not eat the fruit from any of the trees in the garden?" ² "Of course we may eat fruit from the trees in the garden," the woman replied. ³ "It's only the fruit from the tree in the middle of the garden that we are not allowed to eat. God said, 'You must not eat it or even touch it; if you do, you will die.'" ⁴ "You won't die!" the serpent replied to the woman. ⁵ "God knows that your eyes will be opened as soon as you eat it, and you will be like God, knowing both good and evil." ⁶ The woman was convinced. She saw that the tree was beautiful and its fruit looked delicious, and she wanted the wisdom it would give her. So she took some of the fruit and ate it. Then she gave some to her husband, who was with her, and he ate it, too. ⁷ At that moment their eyes were opened, and they suddenly felt shame at their nakedness. So they sewed fig leaves together to cover themselves. ⁸ When the cool evening breezes were blowing, the man and his wife heard the Lord God walking about in the garden. So they hid from the Lord God among the trees. ⁹ Then the Lord God called to the man, "Where are you?" ¹⁰ He replied, "I heard you walking in the garden, so I hid. I was afraid because I was naked." ¹¹ "Who told you that you were naked?" the Lord God asked. "Have you eaten from the tree whose fruit I commanded you not to eat?" ¹² The man replied, "It was the woman you gave me who gave me the fruit, and I ate it." ¹³ Then the Lord God asked the woman, "What have you done?" "The serpent deceived me," she replied. "That's why I ate it." ¹⁴ Then the Lord God said to the serpent, "Because you have done this, you are cursed more than all animals, domestic and wild. You will crawl on your belly, groveling in the dust as long as you live. ¹⁵ And I will cause hostility between you and the woman, and between your offspring and her offspring. He will strike your head, and you will strike his heel." ¹⁶ Then he said to the woman, "I will sharpen the pain of your pregnancy, and in pain you will give birth. And you will desire to control your husband, but he will rule over you." ¹⁷ And to the man he said, "Since you listened to your wife and ate from the tree whose fruit I commanded you not to eat, the ground is cursed because of you. All your life you will struggle to scratch a living from it. ¹⁸ It will grow thorns and thistles for you, though you will eat of its grains. ¹⁹ By the sweat of your brow will you have food to eat until you return to the ground from which you were made. For you were made from dust, and to dust you will return."

PARADISE LOST: GOD'S JUDGMENT

²⁰ Then the man—Adam—named his wife Eve, because she would be the mother of all who live. ²¹ And the Lord God made clothing from animal skins for Adam and his wife. ²² Then the Lord God said, "Look, the human beings have become like us, knowing both good and evil. What if they reach out, take fruit from the tree of life, and eat it? Then they will live forever!" ²³ So the Lord God banished them from the Garden of Eden, and he sent Adam out to cultivate the ground from which he had been made. ²⁴ After sending them out, the Lord God stationed mighty cherubim to the east of the Garden of Eden. And he placed a flaming sword that flashed back and forth to guard the way to the tree of life.

4

CAIN AND ABEL

[1] Now Adam had sexual relations with his wife, Eve, and she became pregnant. When she gave birth to Cain, she said, "With the Lord's help, I have produced a man!" [2] Later she gave birth to his brother and named him Abel. When they grew up, Abel became a shepherd, while Cain cultivated the ground. [3] When it was time for the harvest, Cain presented some of his crops as a gift to the Lord. [4] Abel also brought a gift—the best portions of the firstborn lambs from his flock. The Lord accepted Abel and his gift, [5] but he did not accept Cain and his gift. This made Cain very angry, and he looked dejected. [6] "Why are you so angry?" the Lord asked Cain. "Why do you look so dejected? [7] You will be accepted if you do what is right. But if you refuse to do what is right, then watch out! Sin is crouching at the door, eager to control you. But you must subdue it and be its master." [8] One day Cain suggested to his brother, "Let's go out into the fields." And while they were in the field, Cain attacked his brother, Abel, and killed him. [9] Afterward the Lord asked Cain, "Where is your brother? Where is Abel?" "I don't know," Cain responded. "Am I my brother's guardian?" [10] But the Lord said, "What have you done? Listen! Your brother's blood cries out to me from the ground! [11] Now you are cursed and banished from the ground, which has swallowed your brother's blood. [12] No longer will the ground yield good crops for you, no matter how hard you work! From now on you will be a homeless wanderer on the earth." [13] Cain replied to the Lord, "My punishment is too great for me to bear! [14] You have banished me from the land and from your presence; you have made me a homeless wanderer. Anyone who finds me will kill me!" [15] The Lord replied, "No, for I will give a sevenfold punishment to anyone who kills you." Then the Lord put a mark on Cain to warn anyone who might try to kill him. [16] So Cain left the Lord's presence and settled in the land of Nod, east of Eden.

THE DESCENDANTS OF CAIN

¹⁷ Cain had sexual relations with his wife, and she became pregnant and gave birth to Enoch. Then Cain founded a city, which he named Enoch, after his son. ¹⁸ Enoch had a son named Irad. Irad became the father of Mehujael. Mehujael became the father of Methushael. Methushael became the father of Lamech. ¹⁹ Lamech married two women. The first was named Adah, and the second was Zillah. ²⁰ Adah gave birth to Jabal, who was the first of those who raise livestock and live in tents. ²¹ His brother's name was Jubal, the first of all who play the harp and flute. ²² Lamech's other wife, Zillah, gave birth to a son named Tubal-cain. He became an expert in forging tools of bronze and iron. Tubal-cain had a sister named Naamah. ²³ One day Lamech said to his wives, "Adah and Zillah, hear my voice; listen to me, you wives of Lamech. I have killed a man who attacked me, a young man who wounded me. ²⁴ If someone who kills Cain is punished seven times, then the one who kills me will be punished seventy-seven times!"

THE BIRTH OF SETH

²⁵ Adam had sexual relations with his wife again, and she gave birth to another son. She named him Seth, for she said, "God has granted me another son in place of Abel, whom Cain killed." ²⁶ When Seth grew up, he had a son and named him Enosh. At that time people first began to worship the Lord by name.

5

THE DESCENDANTS OF ADAM

[1] This is the written account of the descendants of Adam. When God created human beings, he made them to be like himself. [2] He created them male and female, and he blessed them and called them "human." [3] When Adam was 130 years old, he became the father of a son who was just like him— in his very image. He named his son Seth. [4] After the birth of Seth, Adam lived another 800 years, and he had other sons and daughters. [5] Adam lived 930 years, and then he died. [6] When Seth was 105 years old, he became the father of Enosh. [7] After the birth of Enosh, Seth lived another 807 years, and he had other sons and daughters. [8] Seth lived 912 years, and then he died. [9] When Enosh was 90 years old, he became the father of Kenan. [10] After the birth of Kenan, Enosh lived another 815 years, and he had other sons and daughters. [11] Enosh lived 905 years, and then he died. [12] When Kenan was 70 years old, he became the father of Mahalalel. [13] After the birth of Mahalalel, Kenan lived another 840 years, and he had other sons and daughters. [14] Kenan lived 910 years, and then he died. [15] When Mahalalel was 65 years old, he became the father of Jared. [16] After the birth of Jared, Mahalalel lived another 830 years, and he had other sons and daughters. [17] Mahalalel lived 895 years, and then he died. [18] When Jared was 162 years old, he became the father of Enoch. [19] After the birth of Enoch, Jared lived another 800 years, and he had other sons and daughters. [20] Jared lived 962 years, and then he died. [21] When Enoch was 65 years old, he became the father of Methuselah. [22] After the birth of Methuselah, Enoch lived in close fellowship with God for another 300 years, and he had other sons and daughters. [23] Enoch lived 365 years, [24] walking in close fellowship with God. Then one day he disappeared, because God took him. [25] When Methuselah was 187 years old, he became the father of Lamech. [26] After the birth of Lamech, Methuselah lived another 782 years, and he had other sons and daughters. [27] Methuselah lived 969 years, and then he died. [28] When Lamech was 182 years old, he became the father of a son. [29] Lamech named his son Noah, for he said, "May he bring us relief from our work and the painful labor of farming this ground that the Lord has cursed." [30] After the birth of Noah, Lamech lived another 595 years, and he had other sons and daughters. [31] Lamech lived 777 years, and then he died. [32] After Noah was 500 years old, he became the father of Shem, Ham, and Japheth.

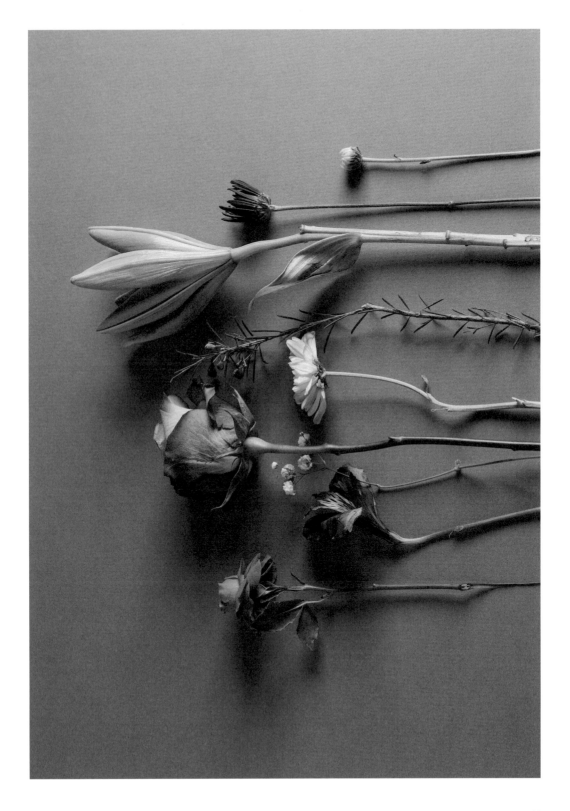

CHAPTER 5

6

A WORLD GONE WRONG

¹ Then the people began to multiply on the earth, and daughters were born to them. ² The sons of God saw the beautiful women and took any they wanted as their wives. ³ Then the Lord said, "My Spirit will not put up with humans for such a long time, for they are only mortal flesh. In the future, their normal lifespan will be no more than 120 years." ⁴ In those days, and for some time after, giant Nephilites lived on the earth, for whenever the sons of God had intercourse with women, they gave birth to children who became the heroes and famous warriors of ancient times. ⁵ The Lord observed the extent of human wickedness on the earth, and he saw that everything they thought or imagined was consistently and totally evil. ⁶ So the Lord was sorry he had ever made them and put them on the earth. It broke his heart. ⁷ And the Lord said, "I will wipe this human race I have created from the face of the earth. Yes, and I will destroy every living thing—all the people, the large animals, the small animals that scurry along the ground, and even the birds of the sky. I am sorry I ever made them." ⁸ But Noah found favor with the Lord.

THE STORY OF NOAH

⁹ This is the account of Noah and his family. Noah was a righteous man, the only blameless person living on earth at the time, and he walked in close fellowship with God. ¹⁰ Noah was the father of three sons: Shem, Ham, and Japheth. ¹¹ Now God saw that the earth had become corrupt and was filled with violence. ¹² God observed all this corruption in the world, for everyone on earth was corrupt. ¹³ So God said to Noah, "I have decided to destroy all living creatures, for they have filled the earth with violence. Yes, I will wipe them all out along with the earth! ¹⁴ Build a large boat from cypress wood and waterproof it with tar, inside and out. Then construct decks and stalls throughout its interior. ¹⁵ Make the boat 450 feet long, 75 feet wide, and 45 feet high. ¹⁶ Leave an 18-inch opening below the roof all the

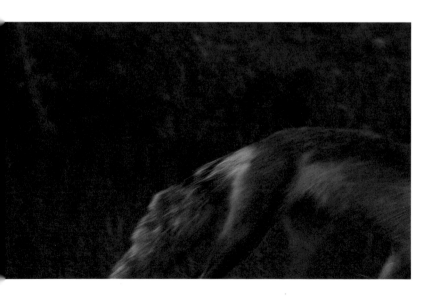

way around the boat. Put the door on the side, and build three decks inside the boat—lower, middle, and upper. 17 Look! I am about to cover the earth with a flood that will destroy every living thing that breathes. Everything on earth will die. 18 But I will confirm my covenant with you. So enter the boat—you and your wife and your sons and their wives. 19 Bring a pair of every kind of animal—a male and a female—into the boat with you to keep them alive during the flood. 20 Pairs of every kind of bird, and every kind of animal, and every kind of small animal that scurries along the ground, will come to you to be kept alive. 21 And be sure to take on board enough food for your family and for all the animals." 22 So Noah did everything exactly as God had commanded him.

7

THE FLOOD COVERS THE EARTH

¹ When everything was ready, the Lord said to Noah, "Go into the boat with all your family, for among all the people of the earth, I can see that you alone are righteous. ² Take with you seven pairs—male and female—of each animal I have approved for eating and for sacrifice, and take one pair of each of the others. ³ Also take seven pairs of every kind of bird. There must be a male and a female in each pair to ensure that all life will survive on the earth after the flood. ⁴ Seven days from now I will make the rains pour down on the earth. And it will rain for forty days and forty nights, until I have wiped from the earth all the living things I have created." ⁵ So Noah did everything as the Lord commanded him. ⁶ Noah was 600 years old when the flood covered the earth. ⁷ He went on board the boat to escape the flood—he and his wife and his sons and their wives. ⁸ With them were all the various kinds of animals—those approved for eating and for sacrifice and those that were not—along with all the birds and the small animals that scurry along the ground. ⁹ They entered the boat in pairs, male and female, just as God had commanded Noah. ¹⁰ After seven days, the waters of the flood came and covered the earth. ¹¹ When Noah was 600 years old, on the seventeenth day of the second month, all the underground waters erupted from the earth,

and the rain fell in mighty torrents from the sky. ¹² The rain continued to fall for forty days and forty nights. ¹³ That very day Noah had gone into the boat with his wife and his sons—Shem, Ham, and Japheth—and their wives. ¹⁴ With them in the boat were pairs of every kind of animal—domestic and wild, large and small—along with birds of every kind. ¹⁵ Two by two they came into the boat, representing every living thing that breathes. ¹⁶ A male and female of each kind entered, just as God had commanded Noah. Then the Lord closed the door behind them. ¹⁷ For forty days the floodwaters grew deeper, covering the ground and lifting the boat high above the earth. ¹⁸ As the waters rose higher and higher above the ground, the boat floated safely on the surface. ¹⁹ Finally, the water covered even the highest mountains on the earth, ²⁰ rising more than twenty-two feet above the highest peaks. ²¹ All the living things on earth died—birds, domestic animals, wild animals, small animals that scurry along the ground, and all the people. ²² Everything that breathed and lived on dry land died. ²³ God wiped out every living thing on the earth—people, livestock, small animals that scurry along the ground, and the birds of the sky. All were destroyed. The only people who survived were Noah and those with him in the boat. ²⁴ And the floodwaters covered the earth for 150 days.

THE FLOOD RECEDES

¹ But God remembered Noah and all the wild animals and livestock with him in the boat. He sent a wind to blow across the earth, and the floodwaters began to recede. ² The underground waters stopped flowing, and the torrential rains from the sky were stopped. ³ So the floodwaters gradually receded from the earth. After 150 days, ⁴ exactly five months from the time the flood began, the boat came to rest on the mountains of Ararat. ⁵ Two and a half months later, as the waters continued to go down, other mountain peaks became visible. ⁶ After another forty days, Noah opened the window he had made in the boat ⁷ and released a raven. The bird flew back and forth until the floodwaters on the earth had dried up. ⁸ He also released a dove to see if the water had receded and it could find dry ground.

⁹ But the dove could find no place to land because the water still covered the ground. So it returned to the boat, and Noah held out his hand and drew the dove back inside. ¹⁰ After waiting another seven days, Noah released the dove again. ¹¹ This time the dove returned to him in the evening with a fresh olive leaf in its beak. Then Noah knew that the floodwaters were almost gone. ¹² He waited another seven days and then released the dove again. This time it did not come back. ¹³ Noah was now 601 years old. On the first day of the new year, ten and a half months after the flood began, the floodwaters had almost dried up from the earth. Noah lifted back the covering of the boat and saw that the surface of the ground was drying. ¹⁴ Two more months went by, and at last the earth was dry! ¹⁵ Then God said to Noah, ¹⁶ "Leave the boat, all of you—you and your wife,

and your sons and their wives. [17] Release all the animals—the birds, the livestock, and the small animals that scurry along the ground—so they can be fruitful and multiply throughout the earth." [18] So Noah, his wife, and his sons and their wives left the boat. [19] And all of the large and small animals and birds came out of the boat, pair by pair. [20] Then Noah built an altar to the Lord, and there he sacrificed as burnt offerings the animals and birds that had been approved for that purpose. [21] And the Lord was pleased with the aroma of the sacrifice and said to himself, "I will never again curse the ground because of the human race, even though everything they think or imagine is bent toward evil from childhood. I will never again destroy all living things. [22] As long as the earth remains, there will be planting and harvest, cold and heat, summer and winter, day and night."

CHAPTER 8

9

GOD CONFIRMS HIS COVENANT

[1] Then God blessed Noah and his sons and told them, "Be fruitful and multiply. Fill the earth. [2] All the animals of the earth, all the birds of the sky, all the small animals that scurry along the ground, and all the fish in the sea will look on you with fear and terror. I have placed them in your power. [3] I have given them to you for food, just as I have given you grain and vegetables. [4] But you must never eat any meat that still has the lifeblood in it. [5] And I will require the blood of anyone who takes another person's life. If a wild animal kills a person, it must die. And anyone who murders a fellow human must die. [6] If anyone takes a human life, that person's life will also be taken by human hands. For God made human beings in his own image. [7] Now be fruitful and multiply, and repopulate the earth." [8] Then God told Noah and his sons, [9] "I hereby confirm my covenant with you and your descendants, [10] and with all the animals that were on the boat with you—the birds, the livestock, and all the wild animals—every living creature on earth. [11] Yes, I am confirming my covenant with you. Never again will floodwaters kill all living creatures; never again will a flood destroy the earth." [12] Then God said, "I am giving you a sign of my covenant with you and with all living creatures, for all generations to come. [13] I have placed my rainbow in the clouds. It is the sign of my covenant with you and with all the earth. [14] When I send clouds over the earth, the rainbow will appear in the clouds, [15] and I will remember my covenant with you and with all living creatures. Never again will the floodwaters destroy all life. [16] When I see the rainbow in the clouds, I will remember the eternal covenant between God and every living creature on earth." [17] Then God said to Noah, "Yes, this rainbow is the sign of the covenant I am confirming with all the creatures on earth."

CHAPTER 9

NOAH'S SONS

[18] The sons of Noah who came out of the boat with their father were Shem, Ham, and Japheth. (Ham is the father of Canaan.) [19] From these three sons of Noah came all the people who now populate the earth. [20] After the flood, Noah began to cultivate the ground, and he planted a vineyard. [21] One day he drank some wine he had made, and he became drunk and lay naked inside his tent. [22] Ham, the father of Canaan, saw that his father was naked and went outside and told his brothers. [23] Then Shem and Japheth took a robe, held it over their shoulders, and backed into the tent to cover their father. As they did this, they looked the other way so they would not see him naked. [24] When Noah woke up from his stupor, he learned what Ham, his youngest son, had done. [25] Then he cursed Canaan, the son of Ham: "May Canaan be cursed! May he be the lowest of servants to his relatives." [26] Then Noah said, "May the Lord, the God of Shem, be blessed, and may Canaan be his servant! [27] May God expand the territory of Japheth! May Japheth share the prosperity of Shem, and may Canaan be his servant." [28] Noah lived another 350 years after the great flood. [29] He lived 950 years, and then he died.

10

¹ This is the account of the families of Shem, Ham, and Japheth, the three sons of Noah. Many children were born to them after the great flood.

DESCENDANTS OF JAPHETH

² The descendants of Japheth were Gomer, Magog, Madai, Javan, Tubal, Meshech, and Tiras. ³ The descendants of Gomer were Ashkenaz, Riphath, and Togarmah. ⁴ The descendants of Javan were Elishah, Tarshish, Kittim, and Rodanim. ⁵ Their descendants became the seafaring peoples that spread out to various lands, each identified by its own language, clan, and national identity.

DESCENDANTS OF HAM

⁶ The descendants of Ham were Cush, Mizraim, Put, and Canaan. ⁷ The descendants of Cush were Seba, Havilah, Sabtah, Raamah, and Sabteca. The descendants of Raamah were Sheba and Dedan. ⁸ Cush was also the ancestor of Nimrod, who was the first heroic warrior on earth. ⁹ Since he was the greatest hunter in the world, his name became proverbial. People would say, "This man is like Nimrod, the greatest hunter in the world." ¹⁰ He built his kingdom in the land of Babylonia, with the cities of Babylon, Erech, Akkad, and Calneh. ¹¹ From there he expanded his territory to Assyria, building the cities of Nineveh, Rehoboth-ir, Calah, ¹² and Resen (the great city located between Nineveh and Calah). ¹³ Mizraim was the ancestor of the Ludites, Anamites, Lehabites, Naphtuhites, ¹⁴ Pathrusites, Casluhites, and the Caphtorites, from whom the Philistines came. ¹⁵ Canaan's oldest son was Sidon, the ancestor of the Sidonians. Canaan was also the ancestor of the Hittites, ¹⁶ Jebusites, Amorites,

Girgashites, [17] Hivites, Arkites, Sinites, [18] Arvadites, Zemarites, and Hamathites. The Canaanite clans eventually spread out, [19] and the territory of Canaan extended from Sidon in the north to Gerar and Gaza in the south, and east as far as Sodom, Gomorrah, Admah, and Zeboiim, near Lasha. [20] These were the descendants of Ham, identified by clan, language, territory, and national identity.

DESCENDANTS OF SHEM

[21] Sons were also born to Shem, the older brother of Japheth. Shem was the ancestor of all the descendants of Eber. [22] The descendants of Shem were Elam, Asshur, Arphaxad, Lud, and Aram. [23] The descendants of Aram were Uz, Hul, Gether, and Mash. [24] Arphaxad was the father of Shelah, and Shelah was the father of Eber. [25] Eber had two sons. The first was named Peleg (which means "division"), for during his lifetime the people of the world were divided into different language groups. His brother's name was Joktan. [26] Joktan was the ancestor of Almodad, Sheleph, Hazarmaveth, Jerah, [27] Hadoram, Uzal, Diklah, [28] Obal, Abimael, Sheba, [29] Ophir, Havilah, and Jobab. All these were descendants of Joktan. [30] The territory they occupied extended from Mesha all the way to Sephar in the eastern mountains. [31] These were the descendants of Shem, identified by clan, language, territory, and national identity.

CONCLUSION

[32] These are the clans that descended from Noah's sons, arranged by nation according to their lines of descent. All the nations of the earth descended from these clans after the great flood.

11

THE TOWER OF BABEL

[1] At one time all the people of the world spoke the same language and used the same words. [2] As the people migrated to the east, they found a plain in the land of Babylonia and settled there. [3] They began saying to each other, "Let's make bricks and harden them with fire." (In this region bricks were used instead of stone, and tar was used for mortar.) [4] Then they said, "Come, let's build a great city for ourselves with a tower that reaches into the sky. This will make us famous and keep us from being scattered all over the world." [5] But the Lord came down to look at the city and the tower the people were building. [6] "Look!" he said. "The people are united, and they all speak the same language. After this, nothing they set out to do will be impossible for them! [7] Come, let's go down and confuse the people with different languages. Then they won't be able to understand each other." [8] In that way, the Lord scattered them all over the world, and they stopped building the city. [9] That is why the city was called Babel, because that is where the Lord confused the people with different languages. In this way he scattered them all over the world.

THE LINE OF DESCENT FROM SHEM TO ABRAM

[10] This is the account of Shem's family. Two years after the great flood, when Shem was 100 years old, he became the father of Arphaxad. [11] After the birth of Arphaxad, Shem lived another 500 years and had other sons and daughters. [12] When Arphaxad was 35 years old, he became the father of Shelah. [13] After the birth of Shelah, Arphaxad lived another 403 years and had other sons and daughters. [14] When Shelah was 30 years old, he became the father of Eber. [15] After the birth of Eber, Shelah lived another 403 years and had other sons and daughters. [16] When Eber was 34 years old, he became the father of Peleg. [17] After the birth of Peleg, Eber lived another 430 years and had other sons and daughters. [18] When Peleg was 30 years old, he became the father of Reu. [19] After the birth of Reu, Peleg lived another 209 years and had other sons and daughters. [20] When Reu was 32 years old, he became the father of Serug. [21] After the birth of Serug, Reu lived another 207 years and had other sons and daughters. [22] When Serug was 30 years old, he became the father of Nahor. [23] After the birth of Nahor, Serug lived another 200 years

and had other sons and daughters. [24] When Nahor was 29 years old, he became the father of Terah. [25] After the birth of Terah, Nahor lived another 119 years and had other sons and daughters. [26] After Terah was 70 years old, he became the father of Abram, Nahor, and Haran.

THE FAMILY OF TERAH

[27] This is the account of Terah's family. Terah was the father of Abram, Nahor, and Haran; and Haran was the father of Lot. [28] But Haran died in Ur of the Chaldeans, the land of his birth, while his father, Terah, was still living. [29] Meanwhile, Abram and Nahor both married. The name of Abram's wife was Sarai, and the name of Nahor's wife was Milcah. (Milcah and her sister Iscah were daughters of Nahor's brother Haran.) [30] But Sarai was unable to become pregnant and had no children. [31] One day Terah took his son Abram, his daughter-in-law Sarai (his son Abram's wife), and his grandson Lot (his son Haran's child) and moved away from Ur of the Chaldeans. He was headed for the land of Canaan, but they stopped at Haran and settled there. [32] Terah lived for 205 years and died while still in Haran.

12

THE CALL OF ABRAM

[1] The Lord had said to Abram, "Leave your native country, your relatives, and your father's family, and go to the land that I will show you. [2] I will make you into a great nation. I will bless you and make you famous, and you will be a blessing to others. [3] I will bless those who bless you and curse those who treat you with contempt. All the families on earth will be blessed through you." [4] So Abram departed as the Lord had instructed, and Lot went with him. Abram was seventy-five years old when he left Haran. [5] He took his wife, Sarai, his nephew Lot, and all his wealth—his livestock and all the people he had taken into his household at Haran—and headed for the land of Canaan. When they arrived in Canaan, [6] Abram traveled through the land as far as Shechem. There he set up camp beside the oak of Moreh. At that time, the area was inhabited by Canaanites. [7] Then the Lord appeared to Abram and said, "I will give this land to your descendants." And Abram built an altar there and dedicated it to the Lord, who had appeared to him. [8] After that, Abram traveled south and set up camp in the hill country, with Bethel to the west and Ai to the east. There he built another altar and dedicated it to the Lord, and he worshiped the Lord. [9] Then Abram continued traveling south by stages toward the Negev.

ABRAM AND SARAI IN EGYPT

[10] At that time a severe famine struck the land of Canaan, forcing Abram to go down to Egypt, where he lived as a foreigner. [11] As he was approaching the border of Egypt, Abram said to his wife, Sarai, "Look, you are a very beautiful woman. [12] When the Egyptians see you, they will say, 'This is his wife. Let's kill him; then we can have her!' [13] So please tell them you are my sister. Then they will spare my life and treat me well because of their interest in you." [14] And sure enough, when Abram arrived in Egypt, everyone noticed Sarai's beauty. [15] When the palace officials saw her, they sang her praises to Pharaoh, their king, and Sarai was taken into his palace. [16] Then Pharaoh gave Abram many gifts because of her—sheep, goats, cattle, male and female donkeys, male and female servants, and camels. [17] But the Lord sent terrible plagues upon Pharaoh and his household because of Sarai, Abram's wife. [18] So Pharaoh summoned Abram and accused him sharply. "What have you done to me?" he demanded. "Why didn't you tell me she was your wife? [19] Why did you say, 'She is my sister,' and allow me to take her as my wife? Now then, here is your wife. Take her and get out of here!" [20] Pharaoh ordered some of his men to escort them, and he sent Abram out of the country, along with his wife and all his possessions.

CHAPTER 12

13

ABRAM AND LOT SEPARATE

[1] So Abram left Egypt and traveled north into the Negev, along with his wife and Lot and all that they owned. [2] (Abram was very rich in livestock, silver, and gold.) [3] From the Negev, they continued traveling by stages toward Bethel, and they pitched their tents between Bethel and Ai, where they had camped before. [4] This was the same place where Abram had built the altar, and there he worshiped the Lord again. [5] Lot, who was traveling with Abram, had also become very wealthy with flocks of sheep and goats, herds of cattle, and many tents. [6] But the land could not support both Abram and Lot with all their flocks and herds living so close together. [7] So disputes broke out between the herdsmen of Abram and Lot. (At that time Canaanites and Perizzites were also living in the land.) [8] Finally Abram said to Lot, "Let's not allow this conflict to come between us or our herdsmen. After all, we are close relatives! [9] The whole countryside is open to you. Take your choice of any section of the land you want, and we will separate. If you want the land to the left, then I'll take the land on the right. If you prefer the land on the right, then I'll go to the left." [10] Lot took a long look at the fertile plains of the Jordan Valley in the direction of Zoar. The whole area was well watered everywhere, like the garden of the Lord or the beautiful land of Egypt. (This was before the Lord destroyed Sodom and Gomorrah.) [11] Lot chose for himself the whole Jordan Valley to the east of them. He went there with his flocks and servants and parted company with his uncle Abram. [12] So Abram settled in the land of Canaan, and Lot moved his tents to a place near Sodom and settled among the cities of the plain. [13] But the people of this area were extremely wicked and constantly sinned against the Lord. [14] After Lot had gone, the Lord said to Abram, "Look as far as you can see in every direction—north and south, east and west. [15] I am giving all this land, as far as you can see, to you and your descendants as a permanent possession. [16] And I will give you so many descendants that, like the dust of the earth, they cannot be counted! [17] Go and walk through the land in every direction, for I am giving it to you." [18] So Abram moved his camp to Hebron and settled near the oak grove belonging to Mamre. There he built another altar to the Lord.

14

ABRAM RESCUES LOT

[1] About this time war broke out in the region. King Amraphel of Babylonia, King Arioch of Ellasar, King Kedorlaomer of Elam, and King Tidal of Goiim [2] fought against King Bera of Sodom, King Birsha of Gomorrah, King Shinab of Admah, King Shemeber of Zeboiim, and the king of Bela (also called Zoar). [3] This second group of kings joined forces in Siddim Valley (that is, the valley of the Dead Sea). [4] For twelve years they had been subject to King Kedorlaomer, but in the thirteenth year they rebelled against him. [5] One year later Kedorlaomer and his allies arrived and defeated the Rephaites at Ashteroth-karnaim, the Zuzites at Ham, the Emites at Shaveh-kiriathaim, [6] and the Horites at Mount Seir, as far as El-paran at the edge of the wilderness. [7] Then they turned back and came to En-mishpat (now called Kadesh) and conquered all the territory of the Amalekites, and also the Amorites living in Hazazon-tamar. [8] Then the rebel kings of Sodom, Gomorrah, Admah, Zeboiim, and Bela (also called Zoar) prepared for battle in the valley of the Dead Sea. [9] They fought against King Kedorlaomer of Elam, King Tidal of Goiim, King Amraphel of Babylonia, and King Arioch of Ellasar—four kings against five. [10] As it happened, the valley of the Dead Sea was filled with tar pits. And as the army of the kings of Sodom and Gomorrah fled, some fell into the tar pits, while the rest escaped into the mountains. [11] The victorious invaders then plundered Sodom and Gomorrah and headed for home, taking with them all the spoils of war and the food supplies. [12] They also captured Lot—Abram's nephew who lived in Sodom—and carried off everything he owned. [13] But one of Lot's men escaped and reported everything to Abram the Hebrew, who was living near the oak grove belonging to Mamre the Amorite. Mamre and his relatives, Eshcol and Aner, were Abram's allies. [14] When Abram heard that his nephew Lot had been captured, he mobilized the 318 trained men who had been born into his household. Then he pursued Kedorlaomer's army until he caught up with them at Dan. [15] There he divided his men and attacked during the night. Kedorlaomer's army fled, but Abram chased them as far as Hobah, north of Damascus. [16] Abram recovered all the goods that had been taken, and he brought back his nephew Lot with his possessions and all the women and other captives.

CHAPTER 14

MELCHIZEDEK BLESSES ABRAM

[17]After Abram returned from his victory over Kedorlaomer and all his allies, the king of Sodom went out to meet him in the valley of Shaveh (that is, the King's Valley). [18] And Melchizedek, the king of Salem and a priest of God Most High, brought Abram some bread and wine. [19] Melchizedek blessed Abram with this blessing: "Blessed be Abram by God Most High, Creator of heaven and earth. [20] And blessed be God Most High, who has defeated your enemies for you." Then Abram gave Melchizedek a tenth of all the goods he had recovered. [21] The king of Sodom said to Abram, "Give back my people who were captured. But you may keep for yourself all the goods you have recovered." [22] Abram replied to the king of Sodom, "I solemnly swear to the Lord, God Most High, Creator of heaven and earth, [23] that I will not take so much as a single thread or sandal thong from what belongs to you. Otherwise you might say, 'I am the one who made Abram rich.' [24] I will accept only what my young warriors have already eaten, and I request that you give a fair share of the goods to my allies—Aner, Eshcol, and Mamre."

15

THE LORD'S COVENANT PROMISE TO ABRAM

[1] Some time later, the Lord spoke to Abram in a vision and said to him, "Do not be afraid, Abram, for I will protect you, and your reward will be great." [2] But Abram replied, "O Sovereign Lord, what good are all your blessings when I don't even have a son? Since you've given me no children, Eliezer of Damascus, a servant in my household, will inherit all my wealth. [3] You have given me no descendants of my own, so one of my servants will be my heir." [4] Then the Lord said to him, "No, your servant will not be your heir, for you will have a son of your own who will be your heir." [5] Then the Lord took Abram outside and said to him, "Look up into the sky and count the stars if you can. That's how many descendants you will have!" [6] And Abram believed the Lord, and the Lord counted him as righteous because of his faith. [7] Then the Lord told him, "I am the Lord who brought you out of Ur of the Chaldeans to give you this land as your possession." [8] But Abram replied, "O Sovereign Lord, how can I be sure that I will actually possess it?" [9] The Lord told him, "Bring me a three-year-old heifer, a three-year-old female goat, a three-year-old ram, a turtledove, and a young pigeon." [10] So Abram presented all these to him and killed them. Then he cut each animal down the middle and laid the halves side by side; he did not, however, cut the birds in half. [11] Some vultures swooped down to eat the carcasses, but Abram chased them away. [12] As the sun was going down, Abram fell into a deep sleep, and a terrifying darkness came down over him. [13] Then the Lord said to Abram, "You can be sure that your descendants will be strangers in a foreign land, where they will be oppressed as slaves for 400 years. [14] But I will punish the nation that enslaves them, and in the end they will come away with great wealth. [15] (As for you, you will die in peace and be buried at a ripe old age.) [16] After four generations your descendants will return here to this land, for the sins of the Amorites do not yet warrant their destruction." [17] After the sun went down and darkness fell, Abram saw a smoking firepot and a flaming torch pass between the halves of the carcasses. [18] So the Lord made a covenant with Abram that day and said, "I have given this land to your descendants, all the way from the border of Egypt to the great Euphrates River— [19] the land now occupied by the Kenites, Kenizzites, Kadmonites, [20] Hittites, Perizzites, Rephaites, [21] Amorites, Canaanites, Girgashites, and Jebusites."

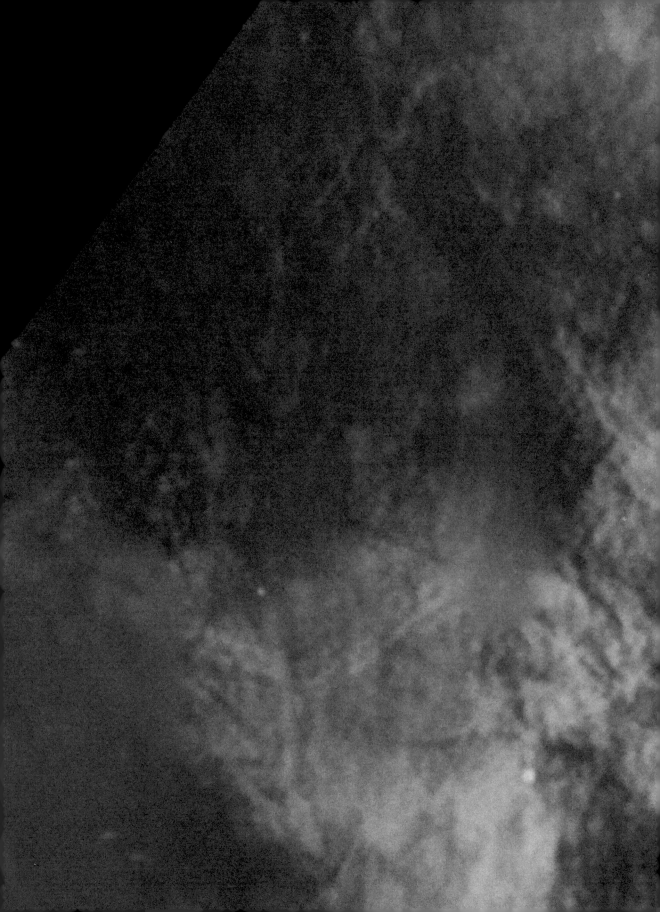

CHAPTER 15

16

THE BIRTH OF ISHMAEL

[1] Now Sarai, Abram's wife, had not been able to bear children for him. But she had an Egyptian servant named Hagar. [2] So Sarai said to Abram, "The Lord has prevented me from having children. Go and sleep with my servant. Perhaps I can have children through her." And Abram agreed with Sarai's proposal. [3] So Sarai, Abram's wife, took Hagar the Egyptian servant and gave her to Abram as a wife. (This happened ten years after Abram had settled in the land of Canaan.) [4] So Abram had sexual relations with Hagar, and she became pregnant. But when Hagar knew she was pregnant, she began to treat her mistress, Sarai, with contempt. [5] Then Sarai said to Abram, "This is all your fault! I put my servant into your arms, but now that she's pregnant she treats me with contempt. The Lord will show who's wrong—you or me!" [6] Abram replied, "Look, she is your servant, so deal with her as you see fit." Then Sarai treated Hagar so harshly that she finally ran away. [7] The angel of the Lord found Hagar beside a spring of water in the wilderness, along the road to Shur. [8] The angel said to her, "Hagar, Sarai's servant, where have you come from, and where are you going?" "I'm running away from my mistress, Sarai," she replied. [9] The angel of the Lord said to her, "Return to your mistress, and submit to her authority." [10] Then he added, "I will give you more descendants than you can count." [11] And the angel also said, "You are now pregnant and will give birth to a son. You are to name him Ishmael (which means 'God hears'), for the Lord has heard your cry of distress. [12] This son of yours will be a wild man, as untamed as a wild donkey! He will raise his fist against everyone, and everyone will be against him. Yes, he will live in open hostility against all his relatives." [13] Thereafter, Hagar used another name to refer to the Lord, who had spoken to her. She said, "You are the God who sees me." She also said, "Have I truly seen the One who sees me?" [14] So that well was named Beer-lahai-roi (which means "well of the Living One who sees me"). It can still be found between Kadesh and Bered. [15] So Hagar gave Abram a son, and Abram named him Ishmael. [16] Abram was eighty-six years old when Ishmael was born.

CHAPTER 16

17

ABRAM IS NAMED ABRAHAM

¹ When Abram was ninety-nine years old, the Lord appeared to him and said, "I am El-Shaddai—'God Almighty.' Serve me faithfully and live a blameless life. ² I will make a covenant with you, by which I will guarantee to give you countless descendants." ³ At this, Abram fell face down on the ground. Then God said to him, ⁴ "This is my covenant with you: I will make you the father of a multitude of nations! ⁵ What's more, I am changing your name. It will no longer be Abram. Instead, you will be called Abraham, for you will be the father of many nations. ⁶ I will make you extremely fruitful. Your descendants will become many nations, and kings will be among them! ⁷ I will confirm my covenant with you and your descendants after you, from generation to generation. This is the everlasting covenant: I will always be your God and the God of your descendants after you. ⁸ And I will give the entire land of Canaan, where you now live as a foreigner, to you and your descendants. It will be their possession forever, and I will be their God."

THE MARK OF THE COVENANT

⁹ Then God said to Abraham, "Your responsibility is to obey the terms of the covenant. You and all your descendants have this continual responsibility. ¹⁰ This is the covenant that you and your descendants must keep: Each male among you must be circumcised. ¹¹ You must cut off the flesh of your foreskin as a sign of the covenant between me and you. ¹² From generation to generation, every male child must be circumcised on the eighth day after his birth. This applies not only to members of your family but also to the servants born in your household and the foreign-born servants whom you have purchased. ¹³ All must be circumcised. Your bodies will bear the mark of my everlasting covenant. ¹⁴ Any male who fails to be circumcised will be cut off from the covenant family for breaking the covenant."

SARAI IS NAMED SARAH

[15] Then God said to Abraham, "Regarding Sarai, your wife—her name will no longer be Sarai. From now on her name will be Sarah. [16] And I will bless her and give you a son from her! Yes, I will bless her richly, and she will become the mother of many nations. Kings of nations will be among her descendants." [17] Then Abraham bowed down to the ground, but he laughed to himself in disbelief. "How could I become a father at the age of 100?" he thought. "And how can Sarah have a baby when she is ninety years old?" [18] So Abraham said to God, "May Ishmael live under your special blessing!" [19] But God replied, "No—Sarah, your wife, will give birth to a son for you. You will name him Isaac, and I will confirm my covenant with him and his descendants as an everlasting covenant. [20] As for Ishmael, I will bless him also, just as you have asked. I will make him extremely fruitful and multiply his descendants. He will become the father of twelve princes, and I will make him a great nation. [21] But my covenant will be confirmed with Isaac, who will be born to you and Sarah about this time next year." [22] When God had finished speaking, he left Abraham.

[23] On that very day Abraham took his son, Ishmael, and every male in his household, including those born there and those he had bought. Then he circumcised them, cutting off their foreskins, just as God had told him. [24] Abraham was ninety-nine years old when he was circumcised, [25] and Ishmael, his son, was thirteen. [26] Both Abraham and his son, Ishmael, were circumcised on that same day, [27] along with all the other men and boys of the household, whether they were born there or bought as servants. All were circumcised with him.

18

A SON IS PROMISED TO SARAH

[1] The Lord appeared again to Abraham near the oak grove belonging to Mamre. One day Abraham was sitting at the entrance to his tent during the hottest part of the day. [2] He looked up and noticed three men standing nearby. When he saw them, he ran to meet them and welcomed them, bowing low to the ground. [3] "My lord," he said, "if it pleases you, stop here for a while. [4] Rest in the shade of this tree while water is brought to wash your feet. [5] And since you've honored your servant with this visit, let me prepare some food to refresh you before you continue on your journey." "All right," they said. "Do as you have said." [6] So Abraham ran back to the tent and said to Sarah, "Hurry! Get three large measures of your best flour, knead it into dough, and bake some bread." [7] Then Abraham ran out to the herd and chose a tender calf and gave it to his servant, who quickly prepared it. [8] When the food was ready, Abraham took some yogurt and milk and the roasted meat, and he served it to the men. As they ate, Abraham waited on them in the shade of the trees. [9] "Where is Sarah, your wife?" the visitors asked. "She's inside the tent," Abraham replied. [10] Then one of them said, "I will return to you about this time next year, and your wife, Sarah, will have a son!" Sarah was listening to this conversation from the tent. [11] Abraham and Sarah were both very old by this time, and Sarah was long past the age of having children. [12] So she laughed silently to herself and said, "How could a worn-out woman like me enjoy such pleasure, especially when my master—my husband—is also so old?" [13] Then the Lord said to Abraham, "Why did Sarah laugh? Why did she say, 'Can an old woman like me have a baby?' [14] Is anything too hard for the Lord? I will return about this time next year, and Sarah will have a son." [15] Sarah was afraid, so she denied it, saying, "I didn't laugh." But the Lord said, "No, you did laugh."

CHAPTER 18

ABRAHAM INTERCEDES FOR SODOM

[16] Then the men got up from their meal and looked out toward Sodom. As they left, Abraham went with them to send them on their way. [17] "Should I hide my plan from Abraham?" the Lord asked. [18] "For Abraham will certainly become a great and mighty nation, and all the nations of the earth will be blessed through him. [19] I have singled him out so that he will direct his sons and their families to keep the way of the Lord by doing what is right and just. Then I will do for Abraham all that I have promised." [20] So the Lord told Abraham, "I have heard a great outcry from Sodom and Gomorrah, because their sin is so flagrant. [21] I am going down to see if their actions are as wicked as I have heard. If not, I want to know." [22] The other men turned and headed toward Sodom, but the Lord remained with Abraham. [23] Abraham approached him and said, "Will you sweep away both the righteous and the wicked? [24] Suppose you find fifty righteous people living there in the city—will you still sweep it away and not spare it for their sakes? [25] Surely you wouldn't do such a thing, destroying the righteous along with the wicked. Why, you would be treating the righteous and the wicked exactly the same! Surely you wouldn't do that! Should not the Judge of all the earth do what is right?" [26] And the Lord replied, "If I find fifty righteous people in Sodom, I will spare the entire city for their sake." [27] Then Abraham spoke again. "Since I have begun, let me speak further to my Lord, even though I am but dust and ashes. [28] Suppose there are only forty-five righteous people rather than fifty? Will you destroy the whole city for lack of five?" And the Lord said, "I will not destroy it if I find forty-five righteous people there." [29] Then Abraham pressed his request further. "Suppose there are only forty?" And the Lord replied, "I will not destroy it for the sake of the forty." [30] "Please don't be angry, my Lord," Abraham pleaded. "Let me speak—suppose only thirty righteous people are found?" And the Lord replied, "I will not destroy it if I find thirty." [31] Then Abraham said, "Since I have dared to speak to the Lord, let me continue—suppose there are only twenty?" And the Lord replied, "Then I will not destroy it for the sake of the twenty." [32] Finally, Abraham said, "Lord, please don't be angry with me if I speak one more time. Suppose only ten are found there?" And the Lord replied, "Then I will not destroy it for the sake of the ten." [33] When the Lord had finished his conversation with Abraham, he went on his way, and Abraham returned to his tent.

19

SODOM AND GOMORRAH DESTROYED

[1] That evening the two angels came to the entrance of the city of Sodom. Lot was sitting there, and when he saw them, he stood up to meet them. Then he welcomed them and bowed with his face to the ground. [2] "My lords," he said, "come to my home to wash your feet, and be my guests for the night. You may then get up early in the morning and be on your way again." "Oh no," they replied. "We'll just spend the night out here in the city square." [3] But Lot insisted, so at last they went home with him. Lot prepared a feast for them, complete with fresh bread made without yeast, and they ate. [4] But before they retired for the night, all the men of Sodom, young and old, came from all over the city and surrounded the house. [5] They shouted to Lot, "Where are the men who came to spend the night with you? Bring them out to us so we can have sex with them!" [6] So Lot stepped outside to talk to them, shutting the door behind him. [7] "Please, my brothers," he begged, "don't do such a wicked thing. [8] Look, I have two virgin daughters. Let me bring them out to you, and you can do with them as you wish. But please, leave these men alone, for they are my guests and are under my protection." [9] "Stand back!" they shouted. "This fellow came to town as an outsider, and now he's acting like our judge! We'll treat you far worse than those other men!" And they lunged toward Lot to break down the door. [10] But the two angels reached out, pulled Lot into the house, and bolted the door. [11] Then they blinded all the men, young and old, who were at the door of the house, so they gave up trying to get inside. [12] Meanwhile, the angels questioned Lot. "Do you have any other relatives here in the city?" they asked. "Get them out of this place—your sons-in-law, sons, daughters, or anyone else. [13] For we are about to destroy this city completely. The outcry against this place is so great it has reached the Lord, and he has sent us to destroy it." [14] So Lot rushed out to tell his daughters' fiancés, "Quick, get out of the city! The Lord is about to destroy it." But the young men thought he was only joking. [15] At dawn the next morning the angels became insistent. "Hurry," they said to Lot. "Take your wife and your two daughters who are here. Get out right now, or you will be swept away in the destruction of the city!" [16] When Lot still hesitated, the angels seized his hand and the hands of his wife and two daughters and rushed them to safety outside the city, for the Lord was merciful. [17] When they were safely out of the city, one of the angels ordered, "Run for your lives! And don't look back or stop anywhere in the valley! Escape to the mountains, or you will be swept away!" [18] "Oh no, my lord!" Lot begged. [19] "You have been so gracious to me

and saved my life, and you have shown such great kindness. But I cannot go to the mountains. Disaster would catch up to me there, and I would soon die. [20] See, there is a small village nearby. Please let me go there instead; don't you see how small it is? Then my life will be saved." [21] "All right," the angel said, "I will grant your request. I will not destroy the little village. [22] But hurry! Escape to it, for I can do nothing until you arrive there." (This explains why that village was known as Zoar, which means "little place.") [23] Lot reached the village just as the sun was rising over the horizon. [24] Then the Lord rained down fire and burning sulfur from the sky on Sodom and Gomorrah. [25] He utterly destroyed them, along with the other cities and villages of the plain, wiping out all the people and every bit of vegetation. [26] But Lot's wife looked back as she was following behind him, and she turned into a pillar of salt. [27] Abraham got up early that morning and hurried out to the place where he had stood in the Lord's presence. [28] He looked out across the plain toward Sodom and Gomorrah and watched as columns of smoke rose from the cities like smoke from a furnace. [29] But God had listened to Abraham's request and kept Lot safe, removing him from the disaster that engulfed the cities on the plain.

LOT AND HIS DAUGHTERS

[30] Afterward Lot left Zoar because he was afraid of the people there, and he went to live in a cave in the mountains with his two daughters. [31] One day the older daughter said to her sister, "There are no men left anywhere in this entire area, so we can't get married like everyone else. And our father will soon be too old to have children. [32] Come, let's get him drunk with wine, and then we will have sex with him. That way we will preserve our family line through our father." [33] So that night they got him drunk with wine, and the older daughter went in and had intercourse with her father. He was unaware of her lying down or getting up again. [34] The next morning the older daughter said to her younger sister, "I had sex with our father last night. Let's get him drunk with wine again tonight, and you go in and have sex with him. That way we will preserve our family line through our father." [35] So that night they got him drunk with wine again, and the younger daughter went in and had intercourse with him. As before, he was unaware of her lying down or getting up again. [36] As a result, both of Lot's daughters became pregnant by their own father. [37] When the older daughter gave birth to a son, she named him Moab. He became the ancestor of the nation now known as the Moabites. [38] When the younger daughter gave birth to a son, she named him Ben-ammi. He became the ancestor of the nation now known as the Ammonites.

20

ABRAHAM DECEIVES ABIMELECH

[1] Abraham moved south to the Negev and lived for a while between Kadesh and Shur, and then he moved on to Gerar. While living there as a foreigner, [2] Abraham introduced his wife, Sarah, by saying, "She is my sister." So King Abimelech of Gerar sent for Sarah and had her brought to him at his palace. [3] But that night God came to Abimelech in a dream and told him, "You are a dead man, for that woman you have taken is already married!" [4] But Abimelech had not slept with her yet, so he said, "Lord, will you destroy an innocent nation? [5] Didn't Abraham tell me, 'She is my sister'? And she herself said, 'Yes, he is my brother.' I acted in complete innocence! My hands are clean." [6] In the dream God responded, "Yes, I know you are innocent. That's why I kept you from sinning against me, and why I did not let you touch her. [7] Now return the woman to her husband, and he will pray for you, for he is a prophet. Then you will live. But if you don't return her to him, you can be sure that you and all your people will die." [8] Abimelech got up early the next morning and quickly called all his servants together. When he told them what had happened, his men were terrified. [9] Then Abimelech called for Abraham. "What have you done to us?" he demanded. "What crime have I committed that deserves treatment like this, making me and my kingdom guilty of this great sin? No one should ever do what you have done! [10] Whatever possessed you to do such a thing?" [11] Abraham replied, "I thought, 'This is a godless place. They will want my wife and will kill me to get her.' [12] And she really is my sister, for we both have the same father, but different mothers. And I married her. [13] When God called me to leave my father's home and to travel from place to place, I told her, 'Do me a favor. Wherever we go, tell the people that I am your brother.'" [14] Then Abimelech took some of his sheep and goats, cattle, and male and female servants, and he presented them to Abraham. He also returned his wife, Sarah, to him. [15] Then Abimelech said, "Look over my land and choose any place where you would like to live." [16] And he said to Sarah, "Look, I am giving your 'brother' 1,000 pieces of silver in the presence of all these witnesses. This is to compensate you for any wrong I may have done to you. This will settle any claim against me, and your reputation is cleared." [17] Then Abraham prayed to God, and God healed Abimelech, his wife, and his female servants, so they could have children. [18] For the Lord had caused all the women to be infertile because of what happened with Abraham's wife, Sarah.

21

THE BIRTH OF ISAAC

[1] The Lord kept his word and did for Sarah exactly what he had promised. [2] She became pregnant, and she gave birth to a son for Abraham in his old age. This happened at just the time God had said it would. [3] And Abraham named their son Isaac. [4] Eight days after Isaac was born, Abraham circumcised him as God had commanded. [5] Abraham was 100 years old when Isaac was born. [6] And Sarah declared, "God has brought me laughter. All who hear about this will laugh with me. [7] Who would have said to Abraham that Sarah would nurse a baby? Yet I have given Abraham a son in his old age!"

HAGAR AND ISHMAEL ARE SENT AWAY

[8] When Isaac grew up and was about to be weaned, Abraham prepared a huge feast to celebrate the occasion. [9] But Sarah saw Ishmael—the son of Abraham and her Egyptian servant Hagar—making fun of her son, Isaac. [10] So she turned to Abraham and demanded, "Get rid of that slave woman and her son. He is not going to share the inheritance with my son, Isaac. I won't have it!" [11] This upset Abraham very much because Ishmael was his son. [12] But God told Abraham, "Do not be upset over the boy and your servant. Do whatever Sarah tells you, for Isaac is the son through whom your descendants will be counted. [13] But I will also make a nation of the descendants of Hagar's son because he is your son, too." [14] So Abraham got up early the next morning, prepared food and a container of water, and strapped them on Hagar's shoulders. Then he sent her away with their son, and she wandered aimlessly in the wilderness of Beersheba. [15] When the water was gone, she put the boy in the shade of a bush. [16] Then she went and sat down by herself about a hundred yards away. "I don't want to watch the boy die," she said, as she burst into tears. [17] But God heard the boy crying, and the angel of God called to Hagar from heaven, "Hagar, what's wrong? Do not be afraid! God has heard the boy crying as he lies there. [18] Go to him and comfort him, for I will make a great nation from his descendants." [19] Then God opened Hagar's eyes, and she saw a well full of water. She quickly filled her water container and gave the boy a drink. [20] And God was with the boy as he grew up in the wilderness. He became a skillful archer, [21] and he settled in the wilderness of Paran. His mother arranged for him to marry a woman from the land of Egypt.

ABRAHAM'S COVENANT WITH ABIMELECH

[22] About this time, Abimelech came with Phicol, his army commander, to visit Abraham. "God is obviously with you, helping you in everything you do," Abimelech said. [23] "Swear to me in God's name that you will never deceive me, my children, or any of my descendants. I have been loyal to you, so now swear that you will be loyal to me and to this country where you are living as a foreigner." [24] Abraham replied, "Yes, I swear to it!" [25] Then Abraham complained to Abimelech about a well that Abimelech's servants had taken by force from Abraham's servants. [26] "This is the first I've heard of it," Abimelech answered. "I have no idea who is responsible. You have never complained about this before." [27] Abraham then gave some of his sheep, goats, and cattle to Abimelech, and they made a treaty. [28] But Abraham also took seven additional female lambs and set them off by themselves. [29] Abimelech asked, "Why have you set these seven apart from the others?" [30] Abraham replied, "Please accept these seven lambs to show your agreement that I dug this well." [31] Then he named the place Beersheba (which means "well of the oath"), because that was where they had sworn the oath. [32] After making their covenant at Beersheba, Abimelech left with Phicol, the commander of his army, and they returned home to the land of the Philistines. [33] Then Abraham planted a tamarisk tree at Beersheba, and there he worshiped the Lord, the Eternal God. [34] And Abraham lived as a foreigner in Philistine country for a long time.

22

ABRAHAM'S FAITH TESTED

[1] Some time later, God tested Abraham's faith. "Abraham!" God called. "Yes," he replied. "Here I am." [2] "Take your son, your only son—yes, Isaac, whom you love so much—and go to the land of Moriah. Go and sacrifice him as a burnt offering on one of the mountains, which I will show you." [3] The next morning Abraham got up early. He saddled his donkey and took two of his servants with him, along with his son, Isaac. Then he chopped wood for a fire for a burnt offering and set out for the place God had told him about. [4] On the third day of their journey, Abraham looked up and saw the place in the distance. [5] "Stay here with the donkey," Abraham told the servants. "The boy and I will travel a little farther. We will worship there, and then we will come right back." [6] So Abraham placed the wood for the burnt offering on Isaac's shoulders, while he himself carried the fire and the knife. As the two of them walked on together, [7] Isaac turned to Abraham and said, "Father?" "Yes, my son?" Abraham replied. "We have the fire and the wood," the boy said, "but where is the sheep for the burnt offering?" [8] "God will provide a sheep for the burnt offering, my son," Abraham answered. And they both walked on together. [9] When they arrived at the place where God had told him to go, Abraham built an altar and arranged the wood on it. Then he tied his son, Isaac, and laid him on the altar on top of the wood.

[10] And Abraham picked up the knife to kill his son as a sacrifice. [11] At that moment the angel of the Lord called to him from heaven, "Abraham! Abraham!" "Yes," Abraham replied. "Here I am!" [12] "Don't lay a hand on the boy!" the angel said. "Do not hurt him in any way, for now I know that you truly fear God. You have not withheld from me even your son, your only son." [13] Then Abraham looked up and saw a ram caught by its horns in a thicket. So he took the ram and sacrificed it as a burnt offering in place of his son. [14] Abraham named the place Yahweh-Yireh (which means "the Lord will provide"). To this day, people still use that name as a proverb: "On the mountain of the Lord it will be provided." [15] Then the angel of the Lord called again to Abraham from heaven. [16] "This is what the Lord says: Because you have obeyed me and have not withheld even your son, your only

son, I swear by my own name that ¹⁷ I will certainly bless you. I will multiply your descendants beyond number, like the stars in the sky and the sand on the seashore. Your descendants will conquer the cities of their enemies. ¹⁸ And through your descendants all the nations of the earth will be blessed—all because you have obeyed me." ¹⁹ Then they returned to the servants and traveled back to Beersheba, where Abraham continued to live. ²⁰ Soon after this, Abraham heard that Milcah, his brother Nahor's wife, had borne Nahor eight sons. ²¹ The oldest was named Uz, the next oldest was Buz, followed by Kemuel (the ancestor of the Arameans), ²² Kesed, Hazo, Pildash, Jidlaph, and Bethuel. ²³ (Bethuel became the father of Rebekah.) In addition to these eight sons from Milcah, ²⁴ Nahor had four other children from his concubine Reumah. Their names were Tebah, Gaham, Tahash, and Maacah.

23

THE BURIAL OF SARAH

[1] When Sarah was 127 years old, [2] she died at Kiriath-arba (now called Hebron) in the land of Canaan. There Abraham mourned and wept for her. [3] Then, leaving her body, he said to the Hittite elders, [4] "Here I am, a stranger and a foreigner among you. Please sell me a piece of land so I can give my wife a proper burial." [5] The Hittites replied to Abraham, [6] "Listen, my lord, you are an honored prince among us. Choose the finest of our tombs and bury her there. No one here will refuse to help you in this way." [7] Then Abraham bowed low before the Hittites [8] and said, "Since you are willing to help me in this way, be so kind as to ask Ephron son of Zohar [9] to let me buy his cave at Machpelah, down at the end of his field. I will pay the full price in the presence of witnesses, so I will have a permanent burial place for my family." [10] Ephron was sitting there among the others, and he answered Abraham as the others listened, speaking publicly before all the Hittite elders of the town. [11] "No, my lord," he said to Abraham, "please listen to me. I will give you the field and the cave. Here in the presence of my people, I give it to you. Go and bury your dead." [12] Abraham again bowed low before the citizens of the land, [13] and he replied to Ephron as everyone listened. "No, listen to me. I will buy it from you. Let me pay the full price for the field so I can bury my dead there." [14] Ephron answered Abraham, [15] "My lord, please listen to me. The land is worth 400 pieces of silver, but what is that between friends? Go ahead and bury your dead." [16] So Abraham agreed to Ephron's price and paid the amount he had suggested—400 pieces of silver, weighed according to the market standard. The Hittite elders witnessed the transaction. [17] So Abraham bought the plot of land belonging to Ephron at Machpelah, near Mamre. This included the field itself, the cave that was in it, and all the surrounding trees. [18] It was transferred to Abraham as his permanent possession in the presence of the Hittite elders at the city gate. [19] Then Abraham buried his wife, Sarah, there in Canaan, in the cave of Machpelah, near Mamre (also called Hebron). [20] So the field and the cave were transferred from the Hittites to Abraham for use as a permanent burial place.

24

A WIFE FOR ISAAC

[1] Abraham was now a very old man, and the Lord had blessed him in every way. [2] One day Abraham said to his oldest servant, the man in charge of his household, "Take an oath by putting your hand under my thigh. [3] Swear by the Lord, the God of heaven and earth, that you will not allow my son to marry one of these local Canaanite women. [4] Go instead to my homeland, to my relatives, and find a wife there for my son Isaac." [5] The servant asked, "But what if I can't find a young woman who is willing to travel so far from home? Should I then take Isaac there to live among your relatives in the land you came from?" [6] "No!" Abraham responded. "Be careful never to take my son there. [7] For the Lord, the God of heaven, who took me from my father's house and my native land, solemnly promised to give this land to my descendants. He will send his angel ahead of you, and he will see to it that you find a wife there for my son. [8] If she is unwilling to come back with you, then you are free from this oath of mine. But under no circumstances are you to take my son there." [9] So the servant took an oath by putting his hand under the thigh of his master, Abraham. He swore to follow Abraham's instructions. [10] Then he loaded ten of Abraham's camels with all kinds of expensive gifts from his master, and he traveled to distant Aram-naharaim. There he went to the town where Abraham's brother Nahor had settled. [11] He made the camels kneel beside a well just outside the town. It was evening, and the women were coming out to draw water. [12] "O Lord, God of my master, Abraham," he prayed. "Please give me success today, and show unfailing love to my master, Abraham. [13] See, I am standing here beside this spring, and the young women of the town are coming out to draw water. [14] This is my request. I will ask one of them, 'Please give me a drink from your jug.' If she says, 'Yes, have a drink, and I will water your camels, too!'—let her be the one you have selected as Isaac's wife. This is how I will know that you have shown unfailing love to my master." [15] Before he had finished praying, he saw a young woman named Rebekah coming out with her water jug on her shoulder. She was the daughter of Bethuel, who was the son of Abraham's brother Nahor and his wife, Milcah. [16] Rebekah was very beautiful and old enough to be married, but she was still a virgin. She went down to the spring, filled her jug, and came up again. [17] Running over to her, the servant said, "Please give me a little drink of water from your jug." [18] "Yes, my lord," she answered, "have a drink." And she quickly lowered her jug from her shoulder and gave him a drink. [19] When she had given him a drink, she said, "I'll draw water for your camels, too, until they have had enough to drink." [20] So she quickly emptied her jug into the watering trough and ran back to the well to draw water for all his camels. [21] The servant watched her in silence, wondering whether or not the Lord had given him success in his mission. [22] Then at last, when the camels had finished drinking, he took out a gold

ring for her nose and two large gold bracelets for her wrists. ²³ "Whose daughter are you?" he asked. "And please tell me, would your father have any room to put us up for the night?" ²⁴ "I am the daughter of Bethuel," she replied. "My grandparents are Nahor and Milcah. ²⁵ Yes, we have plenty of straw and feed for the camels, and we have room for guests." ²⁶ The man bowed low and worshiped the Lord. ²⁷ "Praise the Lord, the God of my master, Abraham," he said. "The Lord has shown unfailing love and faithfulness to my master, for he has led me straight to my master's relatives." ²⁸ The young woman ran home to tell her family everything that had happened. ²⁹ Now Rebekah had a brother named Laban, who ran out to meet the man at the spring. ³⁰ He had seen the nose-ring and the bracelets on his sister's wrists, and had heard Rebekah tell what the man had said. So he rushed out to the spring, where the man was still standing beside his camels. ³¹ Laban said to him, "Come and stay with us, you who are blessed by the Lord! Why are you standing here outside the town when I have a room all ready for you and a place prepared for the camels?" ³² So the man went home with Laban, and Laban unloaded the camels, gave him straw for their bedding, fed them, and provided water for the man and the camel drivers to wash their feet. ³³ Then food was served. But Abraham's servant said, "I don't want to eat until I have told you why I have come." "All right," Laban said, "tell us." ³⁴ "I am Abraham's servant," he explained. ³⁵ "And the Lord has greatly blessed my master; he has become a wealthy man. The Lord has given him flocks of sheep and goats, herds of cattle, a fortune in silver and gold, and many male and female servants and camels and donkeys. ³⁶ When Sarah, my master's wife, was very old, she gave birth to my master's son, and my master has given him everything he owns. ³⁷ And my master made me take an oath. He said, 'Do not allow my son to marry one of these local Canaanite women. ³⁸ Go instead to my father's house, to my relatives, and find a wife there for my son.' ³⁹ But I said to my master, 'What if I can't find a young woman who is willing to go back with me?' ⁴⁰ He responded, 'The Lord, in whose presence I have lived, will send his angel with you and will make your mission successful. Yes, you must find a wife for my son from among my relatives, from my father's family. ⁴¹ Then you will have fulfilled your obligation. But if you go to my relatives and they refuse to let her go with you, you will be free from my oath.' ⁴² So today when I came to the spring, I prayed this prayer: 'O Lord, God of my master, Abraham, please give me success on this mission. ⁴³ See, I am standing here beside this spring. This is my request. When a young woman comes to draw water, I will say to her, "Please give me a little drink of water from your jug." ⁴⁴ If she says, "Yes, have a drink, and I will draw water for your camels, too," let her be the one you have selected to be the wife of my master's son.' ⁴⁵ Before I had finished praying in my heart, I saw Rebekah coming out with her water jug on her shoulder. She went down to the spring and drew water. So I said to her, 'Please give me a drink.' ⁴⁶ She quickly lowered her jug from her shoulder and said, 'Yes, have a drink, and I will water your camels, too!' So I drank, and then she watered the camels. ⁴⁷ Then I asked, 'Whose daughter are you?'

She replied, 'I am the daughter of Bethuel, and my grandparents are Nahor and Milcah.' So I put the ring on her nose, and the bracelets on her wrists. [48] Then I bowed low and worshiped the Lord. I praised the Lord, the God of my master, Abraham, because he had led me straight to my master's niece to be his son's wife. [49] So tell me—will you or won't you show unfailing love and faithfulness to my master? Please tell me yes or no, and then I'll know what to do next." [50] Then Laban and Bethuel replied, "The Lord has obviously brought you here, so there is nothing we can say. [51] Here is Rebekah; take her and go. Yes, let her be the wife of your master's son, as the Lord has directed." [52] When Abraham's servant heard their answer, he bowed down to the ground and worshiped the Lord. [53] Then he brought out silver and gold jewelry and clothing and presented them to Rebekah. He also gave expensive presents to her brother and mother. [54] Then they ate their meal, and the servant and the men with him stayed there overnight. But early the next morning, Abraham's servant said, "Send me back to my master." [55] "But we want Rebekah to stay with us at least ten days," her brother and mother said. "Then she can go." [56] But he said, "Don't delay me. The Lord has made my mission successful; now send me back so I can return to my master." [57] "Well," they said, "we'll call Rebekah and ask her what she thinks." [58] So they called Rebekah. "Are you willing to go with this man?" they asked her. And she replied, "Yes, I will go." [59] So they said good-bye to Rebekah and sent her away with Abraham's servant and his men. The woman who had been Rebekah's childhood nurse went along with her. [60] They gave her this blessing as she parted: "Our sister, may you become the mother of many millions! May your descendants be strong and conquer the cities of their enemies." [61] Then Rebekah and her servant girls mounted the camels and followed the man. So Abraham's servant took Rebekah and went on his way. [62] Meanwhile, Isaac, whose home was in the Negev, had returned from Beer-lahai-roi. [63] One evening as he was walking and meditating in the fields, he looked up and saw the camels coming. [64] When Rebekah looked up and saw Isaac, she quickly dismounted from her camel. [65] "Who is that man walking through the fields to meet us?" she asked the servant. And he replied, "It is my master." So Rebekah covered her face with her veil. [66] Then the servant told Isaac everything he had done. [67] And Isaac brought Rebekah into his mother Sarah's tent, and she became his wife. He loved her deeply, and she was a special comfort to him after the death of his mother.

25

THE DEATH OF ABRAHAM

[1] Abraham married another wife, whose name was Keturah. [2] She gave birth to Zimran, Jokshan, Medan, Midian, Ishbak, and Shuah. [3] Jokshan was the father of Sheba and Dedan. Dedan's descendants were the Asshurites, Letushites, and Leummites. [4] Midian's sons were Ephah, Epher, Hanoch, Abida, and Eldaah. These were all descendants of Abraham through Keturah. [5] Abraham gave everything he owned to his son Isaac. [6] But before he died, he gave gifts to the sons of his concubines and sent them off to a land in the east, away from Isaac. [7] Abraham lived for 175 years, [8] and he died at a ripe old age, having lived a long and satisfying life. He breathed his last and joined his ancestors in death. [9] His sons Isaac and Ishmael buried him in the cave of Machpelah, near Mamre, in the field of Ephron son of Zohar the Hittite. [10] This was the field Abraham had purchased from the Hittites and where he had buried his wife Sarah. [11] After Abraham's death, God blessed his son Isaac, who settled near Beer-lahai-roi in the Negev.

ISHMAEL'S DESCENDANTS

[12] This is the account of the family of Ishmael, the son of Abraham through Hagar, Sarah's Egyptian servant. [13] Here is a list, by their names and clans, of Ishmael's descendants: The oldest was Nebaioth, followed by Kedar, Adbeel, Mibsam, [14] Mishma, Dumah, Massa, [15] Hadad, Tema, Jetur, Naphish, and Kedemah. [16] These twelve sons of Ishmael became the founders of twelve tribes named after them, listed according to the places they settled and camped. [17] Ishmael lived for 137 years. Then he breathed his last and joined his ancestors in death. [18] Ishmael's descendants occupied the region from Havilah to Shur, which is east of Egypt in the direction of Asshur. There they lived in open hostility toward all their relatives.

THE BIRTHS OF ESAU AND JACOB

[19] This is the account of the family of Isaac, the son of Abraham. [20] When Isaac was forty years old, he married Rebekah, the daughter of Bethuel the Aramean from Paddan-aram and the sister of Laban the Aramean. [21] Isaac pleaded with the Lord on behalf of his wife, because she was unable to have children. The Lord answered Isaac's prayer, and Rebekah became pregnant with twins. [22] But the two children struggled with each other in her womb. So she went to ask the Lord about it. "Why is this happening to me?" she asked. [23] And the Lord told her, "The sons in your womb will become two nations. From the very beginning, the two nations will be rivals. One nation will be stronger than the other; and your older son will serve your younger son." [24] And when the time came to give birth, Rebekah discovered that she did indeed have twins! [25] The first one was very red at birth and covered with thick hair like a fur coat. So they named him Esau. [26] Then the other twin was born with his hand grasping Esau's heel. So they named him Jacob. Isaac was sixty years old when the twins were born.

ESAU SELLS HIS BIRTHRIGHT

[27] As the boys grew up, Esau became a skillful hunter. He was an outdoorsman, but Jacob had a quiet temperament, preferring to stay at home. [28] Isaac loved Esau because he enjoyed eating the wild game Esau brought home, but Rebekah loved Jacob. [29] One day when Jacob was cooking some stew, Esau arrived home from the wilderness exhausted and hungry. [30] Esau said to Jacob, "I'm starved! Give me some of that red stew!" (This is how Esau got his other name, Edom, which means "red.") [31] "All right," Jacob replied, "but trade me your rights as the firstborn son." [32] "Look, I'm dying of starvation!" said Esau. "What good is my birthright to me now?" [33] But Jacob said, "First you must swear that your birthright is mine." So Esau swore an oath, thereby selling all his rights as the firstborn to his brother, Jacob. [34] Then Jacob gave Esau some bread and lentil stew. Esau ate the meal, then got up and left. He showed contempt for his rights as the firstborn.

26

ISAAC DECEIVES ABIMELECH

[1] A severe famine now struck the land, as had happened before in Abraham's time. So Isaac moved to Gerar, where Abimelech, king of the Philistines, lived. [2] The Lord appeared to Isaac and said, "Do not go down to Egypt, but do as I tell you. [3] Live here as a foreigner in this land, and I will be with you and bless you. I hereby confirm that I will give all these lands to you and your descendants, just as I solemnly promised Abraham, your father. [4] I will cause your descendants to become as numerous as the stars of the sky, and I will give them all these lands. And through your descendants all the nations of the earth will be blessed. [5] I will do this because Abraham listened to me and obeyed all my requirements, commands, decrees, and instructions." [6] So Isaac stayed in Gerar. [7] When the men who lived there asked Isaac about his wife, Rebekah, he said, "She is my sister." He was afraid to say, "She is my wife." He thought, "They will kill me to get her, because she is so beautiful." [8] But some time later, Abimelech, king of the Philistines, looked out his window and saw Isaac caressing Rebekah. [9] Immediately, Abimelech called for Isaac and exclaimed, "She is obviously your wife! Why did you say, 'She is my sister'?" "Because I was afraid someone would kill me to get her from me," Isaac replied. [10] "How could you do this to us?" Abimelech exclaimed. "One of my people might easily have taken your wife and slept with her, and you would have made us guilty of great sin." [11] Then Abimelech issued a public proclamation: "Anyone who touches this man or his wife will be put to death!"

CONFLICT OVER WATER RIGHTS

[12] When Isaac planted his crops that year, he harvested a hundred times more grain than he planted, for the Lord blessed him. [13] He became a very rich man, and his wealth continued to grow. [14] He acquired so many flocks of sheep and goats, herds of cattle, and servants that the Philistines became jealous of him. [15] So the Philistines filled up all of Isaac's wells with dirt. These were the wells that had been dug by the servants of his father, Abraham. [16] Finally, Abimelech ordered Isaac to leave the country. "Go somewhere else," he said, "for you have become too powerful for us." [17] So Isaac moved away to the Gerar Valley, where he set up their tents and settled down. [18] He reopened the wells his father had dug, which the Philistines had filled in after Abraham's death. Isaac also restored the names Abraham had given them. [19] Isaac's servants also dug in the Gerar Valley and discovered a well of fresh water. [20] But then the shepherds from Gerar came and claimed the spring. "This is our water," they said, and they argued over it with Isaac's herdsmen. So Isaac named the well Esek (which means "argument"). [21] Isaac's men then dug another well, but again there was a dispute over it. So Isaac named it Sitnah (which means "hostility"). [22] Abandoning that one, Isaac moved on and dug another well. This time there was no dispute over it, so Isaac named the place Rehoboth (which means "open space"), for he said, "At last the Lord has created enough space for us to prosper in this land." [23] From there Isaac moved to Beersheba, [24] where the Lord appeared to him on the night of his arrival. "I am the God of your father, Abraham," he said. "Do not be afraid, for I am with you and will bless you. I will multiply your descendants, and they will become a great nation. I will do this because of my promise to Abraham, my servant." [25] Then Isaac built an altar there and worshiped the Lord. He set up his camp at that place, and his servants dug another well.

ISAAC'S COVENANT WITH ABIMELECH

[26] One day King Abimelech came from Gerar with his adviser, Ahuzzath, and also Phicol, his army commander. [27] "Why have you come here?" Isaac asked. "You obviously hate me, since you kicked me off your land." [28] They replied, "We can plainly see that the Lord is with you. So we want to enter into a sworn treaty with you. Let's make a covenant. [29] Swear that you will not harm us, just as we have never troubled you. We have always treated you well, and we sent you away from us in peace. And now look how the Lord has blessed you!" [30] So Isaac prepared a covenant feast to celebrate the treaty, and they ate and drank together. [31] Early the next morning, they each took a solemn oath not to interfere with each other. Then Isaac sent them home again, and they left him in peace. [32] That very day Isaac's servants came and told him about a new well they had dug. "We've found water!" they exclaimed. [33] So Isaac named the well Shibah (which means "oath"). And to this day the town that grew up there is called Beersheba (which means "well of the oath"). [34] At the age of forty, Esau married two Hittite wives: Judith, the daughter of Beeri, and Basemath, the daughter of Elon. [35] But Esau's wives made life miserable for Isaac and Rebekah.

27

JACOB STEALS ESAU'S BLESSING

[1] One day when Isaac was old and turning blind, he called for Esau, his older son, and said, "My son." "Yes, Father?" Esau replied. [2] "I am an old man now," Isaac said, "and I don't know when I may die. [3] Take your bow and a quiver full of arrows, and go out into the open country to hunt some wild game for me. [4] Prepare my favorite dish, and bring it here for me to eat. Then I will pronounce the blessing that belongs to you, my firstborn son, before I die." [5] But Rebekah overheard what Isaac had said to his son Esau. So when Esau left to hunt for the wild game, [6] she said to her son Jacob, "Listen. I overheard your father say to Esau, [7] 'Bring me some wild game and prepare me a delicious meal. Then I will bless you in the Lord's presence before I die.' [8] Now, my son, listen to me. Do exactly as I tell you. [9] Go out to the flocks, and bring me two fine young goats. I'll use them to prepare your father's favorite dish. [10] Then take the food to your father so he can eat it and bless you before he dies." [11] "But look," Jacob replied to Rebekah, "my brother, Esau, is a hairy man, and my skin is smooth. [12] What if my father touches me? He'll see that I'm trying to trick him, and then he'll curse me instead of blessing me." [13] But his mother replied, "Then let the curse fall on me, my son! Just do what I tell you. Go out and get the goats for me!" [14] So Jacob went out and got the young goats for his mother. Rebekah took them and prepared a delicious meal, just the way Isaac liked it. [15] Then she took Esau's favorite clothes, which were there in the house, and gave them to her younger son, Jacob. [16] She covered his arms and the smooth part of his neck with the skin of the young goats. [17] Then she gave Jacob the delicious meal, including freshly baked bread. [18] So Jacob took the food to his father. "My father?" he said. "Yes, my son," Isaac answered. "Who are you—Esau or Jacob?" [19] Jacob replied, "It's Esau, your firstborn son. I've done as you told me. Here is the wild game. Now sit up and eat it so you can give me your blessing." [20] Isaac asked, "How did you find it so quickly, my son?" "The Lord your God put it in my path!" Jacob replied. [21] Then Isaac said to Jacob, "Come closer so I can touch you and make sure that you really are Esau." [22] So Jacob went closer to his father, and Isaac touched him. "The voice is Jacob's, but the hands are Esau's," Isaac said. [23] But he did not recognize Jacob, because Jacob's hands felt hairy just like Esau's. So Isaac prepared to bless Jacob. [24] "But are you really my son Esau?" he asked. "Yes, I am," Jacob replied. [25] Then Isaac said, "Now, my son, bring me the wild game. Let me eat it, and then I will give you my blessing." So Jacob took the food to his father, and Isaac ate it. He also drank the wine that Jacob served

him. ²⁶ Then Isaac said to Jacob, "Please come a little closer and kiss me, my son." ²⁷ So Jacob went over and kissed him. And when Isaac caught the smell of his clothes, he was finally convinced, and he blessed his son. He said, "Ah! The smell of my son is like the smell of the outdoors, which the Lord has blessed! ²⁸ "From the dew of heaven and the richness of the earth, may God always give you abundant harvests of grain and bountiful new wine. ²⁹ May many nations become your servants, and may they bow down to you. May you be the master over your brothers, and may your mother's sons bow down to you. All who curse you will be cursed, and all who bless you will be blessed." ³⁰ As soon as Isaac had finished blessing Jacob, and almost before Jacob had left his father, Esau returned from his hunt. ³¹ Esau prepared a delicious meal and brought it to his father. Then he said, "Sit up, my father, and eat my wild game so you can give me your blessing." ³² But Isaac asked him, "Who are you?" Esau replied, "It's your son, your firstborn son, Esau." ³³ Isaac began to tremble uncontrollably and said, "Then who just served me wild game? I have already eaten it, and I blessed him just before you came. And yes, that blessing must stand!" ³⁴ When Esau heard his father's words, he let out a loud and bitter cry. "Oh my father, what about me? Bless me, too!" he begged. ³⁵ But Isaac said, "Your brother was here, and he tricked me. He has taken away your blessing." ³⁶ Esau exclaimed, "No wonder his name is Jacob, for now he has cheated me twice. First he took my rights as the firstborn, and now he has stolen my blessing. Oh, haven't you saved even one blessing for me?" ³⁷ Isaac said to Esau, "I have made Jacob your master and have declared that all his brothers will be his servants. I have guaranteed him an abundance of grain and wine—what is left for me to give you, my son?" ³⁸ Esau pleaded, "But do you have only one blessing? Oh my father, bless me, too!" Then Esau broke down and wept. ³⁹ Finally, his father, Isaac, said to him, "You will live away from the richness of the earth, and away from the dew of the heaven above. ⁴⁰ You will live by your sword, and you will serve your brother. But when you decide to break free, you will shake his yoke from your neck."

JACOB FLEES TO PADDAN-ARAM

⁴¹ From that time on, Esau hated Jacob because their father had given Jacob the blessing. And Esau began to scheme: "I will soon be mourning my father's death. Then I will kill my brother, Jacob." ⁴² But Rebekah heard about Esau's plans. So she sent for Jacob and told him, "Listen, Esau is consoling himself by plotting to kill you. ⁴³ So listen carefully, my son. Get ready and flee to my brother, Laban, in Haran. ⁴⁴ Stay there with him until your brother cools off. ⁴⁵ When he calms down and forgets what you have done to him, I will send for you to come back. Why should I lose both of you in one day?" ⁴⁶ Then Rebekah said to Isaac, "I'm sick and tired of these local Hittite women! I would rather die than see Jacob marry one of them."

28

¹ So Isaac called for Jacob, blessed him, and said, "You must not marry any of these Canaanite women. ² Instead, go at once to Paddan-aram, to the house of your grandfather Bethuel, and marry one of your uncle Laban's daughters. ³ May God Almighty bless you and give you many children. And may your descendants multiply and become many nations! ⁴ May God pass on to you and your descendants the blessings he promised to Abraham. May you own this land where you are now living as a foreigner, for God gave this land to Abraham." ⁵ So Isaac sent Jacob away, and he went to Paddan-aram to stay with his uncle Laban, his mother's brother, the son of Bethuel the Aramean. ⁶ Esau knew that his father, Isaac, had blessed Jacob and sent him to Paddan-aram to find a wife, and that he had warned Jacob, "You must not marry a Canaanite woman." ⁷ He also knew that Jacob had obeyed his parents and gone to Paddan-aram. ⁸ It was now very clear to Esau that his father did not like the local Canaanite women. ⁹ So Esau visited his uncle Ishmael's family and married one of Ishmael's daughters, in addition to the wives he already had. His new wife's name was Mahalath. She was the sister of Nebaioth and the daughter of Ishmael, Abraham's son.

JACOB'S DREAM AT BETHEL

[10] Meanwhile, Jacob left Beersheba and traveled toward Haran. [11] At sundown he arrived at a good place to set up camp and stopped there for the night. Jacob found a stone to rest his head against and lay down to sleep. [12] As he slept, he dreamed of a stairway that reached from the earth up to heaven. And he saw the angels of God going up and down the stairway. [13] At the top of the stairway stood the Lord, and he said, "I am the Lord, the God of your grandfather Abraham, and the God of your father, Isaac. The ground you are lying on belongs to you. I am giving it to you and your descendants. [14] Your descendants will be as numerous as the dust of the earth! They will spread out in all directions—to the west and the east, to the north and the south. And all the families of the earth will be blessed through you and your descendants. [15] What's more, I am with you, and I will protect you wherever you go. One day I will bring you back to this land. I will not leave you until I have finished giving you everything I have promised you." [16] Then Jacob awoke from his sleep and said, "Surely the Lord is in this place, and I wasn't even aware of it!" [17] But he was also afraid and said, "What an awesome place this is! It is none other than the house of God, the very gateway to heaven!" [18] The next morning Jacob got up very early. He took the stone he had rested his head against, and he set it upright as a memorial pillar. Then he poured olive oil over it. [19] He named that place Bethel (which means "house of God"), although it was previously called Luz. [20] Then Jacob made this vow: "If God will indeed be with me and protect me on this journey, and if he will provide me with food and clothing, [21] and if I return safely to my father's home, then the Lord will certainly be my God. [22] And this memorial pillar I have set up will become a place for worshiping God, and I will present to God a tenth of everything he gives me."

29

JACOB ARRIVES AT PADDAN-ARAM

[1] Then Jacob hurried on, finally arriving in the land of the east. [2] He saw a well in the distance. Three flocks of sheep and goats lay in an open field beside it, waiting to be watered. But a heavy stone covered the mouth of the well. [3] It was the custom there to wait for all the flocks to arrive before removing the stone and watering the animals. Afterward the stone would be placed back over the mouth of the well. [4] Jacob went over to the shepherds and asked, "Where are you from, my friends?" "We are from Haran," they answered. [5] "Do you know a man there named Laban, the grandson of Nahor?" he asked. "Yes, we do," they replied. [6] "Is he doing well?" Jacob asked. "Yes, he's well," they answered. "Look, here comes his daughter Rachel with the flock now." [7] Jacob said, "Look, it's still broad daylight—too early to round up the animals. Why don't you water the sheep and goats so they can get back out to pasture?" [8] "We can't water the animals until all the flocks have arrived," they replied. "Then the shepherds move the stone from the mouth of the well, and we water all the sheep and goats." [9] Jacob was still talking with them when Rachel arrived with her father's flock, for she was a shepherd. [10] And because Rachel was his cousin—the daughter of Laban, his mother's brother—and because the sheep and goats belonged to his uncle Laban, Jacob went over to the well and moved the stone from its mouth and watered his uncle's flock. [11] Then Jacob kissed Rachel, and he wept aloud. [12] He explained to Rachel that he was her cousin on her father's side—the son of her aunt Rebekah. So Rachel quickly ran and told her father, Laban. [13] As soon as Laban heard that his nephew Jacob had arrived, he ran out to meet him. He embraced and kissed him and brought him home. When Jacob had told him his story, [14] Laban exclaimed, "You really are my own flesh and blood!"

JACOB MARRIES LEAH AND RACHEL

After Jacob had stayed with Laban for about a month, [15] Laban said to him, "You shouldn't work for me without pay just because we are relatives. Tell me how much your wages should be." [16] Now Laban had two daughters. The older daughter was named Leah, and the younger one was Rachel. [17] There was no sparkle in Leah's eyes, but Rachel had a beautiful figure and a lovely face. [18] Since Jacob was in love with Rachel, he told her father, "I'll work for you for seven years if you'll give me Rachel, your younger daughter, as my wife." [19] "Agreed!" Laban replied. "I'd rather give her to you than to anyone else. Stay and work with me." [20] So Jacob worked seven years to pay for Rachel. But his love for her was so strong that it seemed to him but a few days. [21] Finally, the time came for him to marry her. "I have fulfilled my agreement," Jacob said to Laban. "Now give me my wife so I can sleep with her." [22] So Laban invited everyone in the neighborhood and prepared a wedding feast. [23] But that night, when it was dark, Laban took Leah to Jacob, and he slept with her. [24] (Laban had given Leah a servant, Zilpah, to be her maid.) [25] But when Jacob woke up in the morning—it was Leah! "What have you done to me?" Jacob raged at Laban. "I worked seven years for Rachel! Why have you tricked me?" [26] "It's not our custom here to marry off a younger daughter ahead of the firstborn," Laban replied. [27] "But wait until the bridal week is over; then we'll give you Rachel, too—provided you promise to work another seven years for me." [28] So Jacob agreed to work seven more years. A week after Jacob had married Leah, Laban gave him Rachel, too. [29] (Laban gave Rachel a servant, Bilhah, to be her maid.) [30] So Jacob slept with Rachel, too, and he loved her much more than Leah. He then stayed and worked for Laban the additional seven years.

JACOB'S MANY CHILDREN

[31] When the Lord saw that Leah was unloved, he enabled her to have children, but Rachel could not conceive. [32] So Leah became pregnant and gave birth to a son. She named him Reuben, for she said, "The Lord has noticed my misery, and now my husband will love me." [33] She soon became pregnant again and gave birth to another son. She named him Simeon, for she said, "The Lord heard that I was unloved and has given me another son." [34] Then she became pregnant a third time and gave birth to another son. He was named Levi, for she said, "Surely this time my husband will feel affection for me, since I have given him three sons!" [35] Once again Leah became pregnant and gave birth to another son. She named him Judah, for she said, "Now I will praise the Lord!" And then she stopped having children.

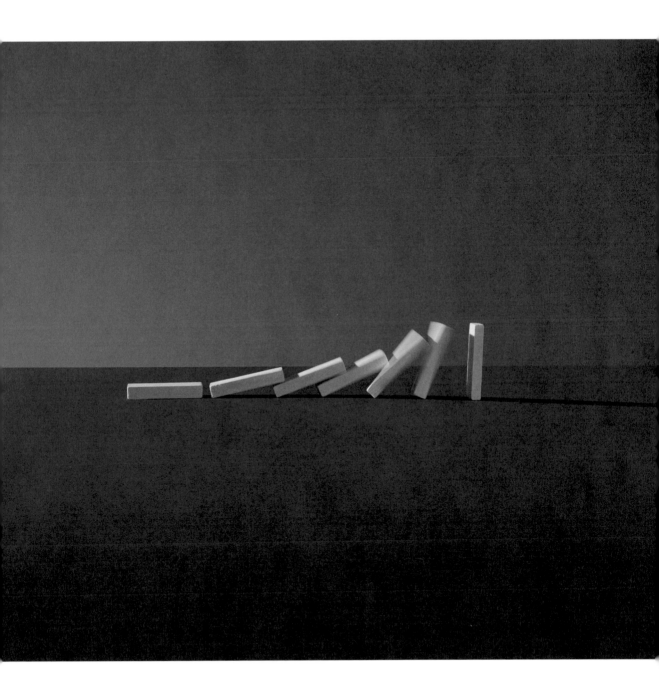

30

¹ When Rachel saw that she wasn't having any children for Jacob, she became jealous of her sister. She pleaded with Jacob, "Give me children, or I'll die!" ² Then Jacob became furious with Rachel. "Am I God?" he asked. "He's the one who has kept you from having children!" ³ Then Rachel told him, "Take my maid, Bilhah, and sleep with her. She will bear children for me, and through her I can have a family, too." ⁴ So Rachel gave her servant, Bilhah, to Jacob as a wife, and he slept with her. ⁵ Bilhah became pregnant and presented him with a son. ⁶ Rachel named him Dan, for she said, "God has vindicated me! He has heard my request and given me a son." ⁷ Then Bilhah became pregnant again and gave Jacob a second son. ⁸ Rachel named him Naphtali, for she said, "I have struggled hard with my sister, and I'm winning!" ⁹ Meanwhile, Leah realized that she wasn't getting pregnant anymore, so she took her servant, Zilpah, and gave her to Jacob as a wife. ¹⁰ Soon Zilpah presented him with a son. ¹¹ Leah named him Gad, for she said, "How fortunate I am!" ¹² Then Zilpah gave Jacob a second son. ¹³ And Leah named him Asher, for she said, "What joy is mine! Now the other women will celebrate with me." ¹⁴ One day during the wheat harvest, Reuben found some mandrakes growing in a field and brought them to his mother, Leah.

Rachel begged Leah, "Please give me some of your son's mandrakes." ¹⁵ But Leah angrily replied, "Wasn't it enough that you stole my husband? Now will you steal my son's mandrakes, too?" Rachel answered, "I will let Jacob sleep with you tonight if you give me some of the mandrakes." ¹⁶ So that evening, as Jacob was coming home from the fields, Leah went out to meet him. "You must come and sleep with me tonight!" she said. "I have paid for you with some mandrakes that my son found." So that night he slept with Leah. ¹⁷ And God answered Leah's prayers. She became pregnant again and gave birth to a fifth son for Jacob. ¹⁸ She named him Issachar, for she said, "God has rewarded me for giving my servant to my husband as a wife." ¹⁹ Then Leah became pregnant again and gave birth to a sixth son for Jacob. ²⁰ She named him Zebulun, for she said, "God has given me a good reward. Now my husband will treat me with respect, for I have given him six sons." ²¹ Later she gave birth to a daughter and named her Dinah. ²² Then God remembered Rachel's plight and answered her prayers by enabling her to have children. ²³ She became pregnant and gave birth to a son. "God has removed my disgrace," she said. ²⁴ And she named him Joseph, for she said, "May the Lord add yet another son to my family."

JACOB'S WEALTH INCREASES

[25] Soon after Rachel had given birth to Joseph, Jacob said to Laban, "Please release me so I can go home to my own country. [26] Let me take my wives and children, for I have earned them by serving you, and let me be on my way. You certainly know how hard I have worked for you." [27] "Please listen to me," Laban replied. "I have become wealthy, for the Lord has blessed me because of you. [28] Tell me how much I owe you. Whatever it is, I'll pay it." [29] Jacob replied, "You know how hard I've worked for you, and how your flocks and herds have grown under my care. [30] You had little indeed before I came, but your wealth has increased enormously. The Lord has blessed you through everything I've done. But now, what about me? When can I start providing for my own family?" [31] "What wages do you want?" Laban asked again. Jacob replied, "Don't give me anything. Just do this one thing, and I'll continue to tend and watch over your flocks. [32] Let me inspect your flocks today and remove all the sheep and goats that are speckled or spotted, along with all the black sheep. Give these to me as my wages. [33] In the future, when you check on the animals you have given me as my wages, you'll see that I have been honest. If you find in my flock any goats without speckles or spots, or any sheep that are not black, you will know that I have stolen them from you." [34] "All right," Laban replied.

"It will be as you say." [35] But that very day Laban went out and removed the male goats that were streaked and spotted, all the female goats that were speckled and spotted or had white patches, and all the black sheep. He placed them in the care of his own sons, [36] who took them a three-days' journey from where Jacob was. Meanwhile, Jacob stayed and cared for the rest of Laban's flock. [37] Then Jacob took some fresh branches from poplar, almond, and plane trees and peeled off strips of bark, making white streaks on them. [38] Then he placed these peeled branches in the watering troughs where the flocks came to drink, for that was where they mated. [39] And when they mated in front of the white-streaked branches, they gave birth to young that were streaked, speckled, and spotted. [40] Jacob separated those lambs from Laban's flock. And at mating time he turned the flock to face Laban's animals that were streaked or black. This is how he built his own flock instead of increasing Laban's. [41] Whenever the stronger females were ready to mate, Jacob would place the peeled branches in the watering troughs in front of them. Then they would mate in front of the branches. [42] But he didn't do this with the weaker ones, so the weaker lambs belonged to Laban, and the stronger ones were Jacob's. [43] As a result, Jacob became very wealthy, with large flocks of sheep and goats, female and male servants, and many camels and donkeys.

31

JACOB FLEES FROM LABAN

[1] But Jacob soon learned that Laban's sons were grumbling about him. "Jacob has robbed our father of everything!" they said. "He has gained all his wealth at our father's expense." [2] And Jacob began to notice a change in Laban's attitude toward him. [3] Then the Lord said to Jacob, "Return to the land of your father and grandfather and to your relatives there, and I will be with you." [4] So Jacob called Rachel and Leah out to the field where he was watching his flock. [5] He said to them, "I have noticed that your father's attitude toward me has changed. But the God of my father has been with me. [6] You know how hard I have worked for your father, [7] but he has cheated me, changing my wages ten times. But God has not allowed him to do me any harm. [8] For if he said, 'The speckled animals will be your wages,' the whole flock began to produce speckled young. And when he changed his mind and said, 'The striped animals will be your wages,' then the whole flock produced striped young. [9] In this way, God has taken your father's animals and given them to me. [10] One time during the mating season, I had a dream and saw that the male goats mating with the females were streaked, speckled, and spotted. [11] Then in my dream, the angel of God said to me, 'Jacob!' And I replied, 'Yes, here I am.' [12] The angel said, 'Look up, and you will see that only the streaked, speckled, and spotted males are mating with the females of your flock. For I have seen how Laban has treated you. [13] I am the God who appeared to you at Bethel, the place where you anointed the pillar of stone and made your vow to me. Now get ready and leave this country and return to the land of your birth.'" [14] Rachel and Leah responded, "That's fine with us! We won't inherit any of our father's wealth anyway. [15] He has reduced our rights to those of foreign women. And after he sold us, he wasted the money you paid him for us. [16] All the wealth God has given you from our father legally belongs to us and our children. So go ahead and do whatever God has told you." [17] So Jacob put his wives and children on camels, [18] and he drove all his livestock in front of him. He packed all the belongings he had acquired in Paddan-aram and set out for the land of Canaan, where his father, Isaac, lived. [19] At the time they left, Laban was some distance away, shearing his sheep. Rachel stole her father's household idols and took them with her. [20] Jacob outwitted Laban the Aramean, for they set out secretly and never told Laban they were leaving. [21] So Jacob took all his possessions with him and crossed the Euphrates River, heading for the hill country of Gilead.

LABAN PURSUES JACOB

²² Three days later, Laban was told that Jacob had fled. ²³ So he gathered a group of his relatives and set out in hot pursuit. He caught up with Jacob seven days later in the hill country of Gilead. ²⁴ But the previous night God had appeared to Laban the Aramean in a dream and told him, "I'm warning you—leave Jacob alone!" ²⁵ Laban caught up with Jacob as he was camped in the hill country of Gilead, and he set up his camp not far from Jacob's. ²⁶ "What do you mean by deceiving me like this?" Laban demanded. "How dare you drag my daughters away like prisoners of war? ²⁷ Why did you slip away secretly? Why did you deceive me? And why didn't you say you wanted to leave? I would have given you a farewell feast, with singing and music, accompanied by tambourines and harps. ²⁸ Why didn't you let me kiss my daughters and grandchildren and tell them good-bye? You have acted very foolishly! ²⁹ I could destroy you, but the God of your father appeared to me last night and warned me, 'Leave Jacob alone!' ³⁰ I can understand your feeling that you must go, and your intense longing for your father's home. But why have you stolen my gods?" ³¹ "I rushed away because I was afraid," Jacob answered. "I thought you would take your daughters from me by force. ³² But as for your gods, see if you can find them, and let the person who has taken them die! And if you find anything else that belongs to you, identify it before all these relatives of ours, and I will give it back!" But Jacob did not know that Rachel had stolen the household idols. ³³ Laban went first into Jacob's tent to search there, then into Leah's, and then the tents of the two servant wives—but he found nothing. Finally, he went into

Rachel's tent. ³⁴ But Rachel had taken the household idols and hidden them in her camel saddle, and now she was sitting on them. When Laban had thoroughly searched her tent without finding them, ³⁵ she said to her father, "Please, sir, forgive me if I don't get up for you. I'm having my monthly period." So Laban continued his search, but he could not find the household idols. ³⁶ Then Jacob became very angry, and he challenged Laban. "What's my crime?" he demanded. "What have I done wrong to make you chase after me as though I were a criminal? ³⁷ You have rummaged through everything I own. Now show me what you found that belongs to you! Set it out here in front of us, before our relatives, for all to see. Let them judge between us! ³⁸ For twenty years I have been with you, caring for your flocks. In all that time your sheep and goats never miscarried. In all those years I never used a single ram of yours for food. ³⁹ If any were attacked and killed by wild animals, I never showed you the carcass and asked you to reduce the count of your flock. No, I took the loss myself! You made me pay for every stolen animal, whether it was taken in broad daylight or in the dark of night. ⁴⁰ I worked for you through the scorching heat of the day and through cold and sleepless nights. ⁴¹ Yes, for twenty years I slaved in your house! I worked for fourteen years earning your two daughters, and then six more years for your flock. And you changed my wages ten times! ⁴² In fact, if the God of my father had not been on my side—the God of Abraham and the fearsome God of Isaac—you would have sent me away empty-handed. But God has seen your abuse and my hard work. That is why he appeared to you last night and rebuked you!"

JACOB'S TREATY WITH LABAN

[43] Then Laban replied to Jacob, "These women are my daughters, these children are my grandchildren, and these flocks are my flocks—in fact, everything you see is mine. But what can I do now about my daughters and their children? [44] So come, let's make a covenant, you and I, and it will be a witness to our commitment." [45] So Jacob took a stone and set it up as a monument. [46] Then he told his family members, "Gather some stones." So they gathered stones and piled them in a heap. Then Jacob and Laban sat down beside the pile of stones to eat a covenant meal. [47] To commemorate the event, Laban called the place Jegar-sahadutha (which means "witness pile" in Aramaic), and Jacob called it Galeed (which means "witness pile" in Hebrew). [48] Then Laban declared, "This pile of stones will stand as a witness to remind us of the covenant we have made today." This explains why it was called Galeed—"Witness Pile." [49] But it was also called Mizpah (which means "watchtower"), for Laban said, "May the Lord keep watch between us to make sure that we keep this covenant when we are out of each other's sight. [50] If you mistreat my daughters or if you marry other wives, God will see it even if no one else does. He is a witness to this covenant between us." [51] "See this pile of stones," Laban continued, "and see this monument I have set between us. [52] They stand between us as witnesses of our vows. I will never pass this pile of stones to harm you, and you must never pass these stones or this monument to harm me. [53] I call on the God of our ancestors—the God of your grandfather Abraham and the God of my grandfather Nahor—to serve as a judge between us." So Jacob took an oath before the fearsome God of his father, Isaac, to respect the boundary line. [54] Then Jacob offered a sacrifice to God there on the mountain and invited everyone to a covenant feast. After they had eaten, they spent the night on the mountain. [55] Laban got up early the next morning, and he kissed his grandchildren and his daughters and blessed them. Then he left and returned home.

32

¹ As Jacob started on his way again, angels of God came to meet him. ² When Jacob saw them, he exclaimed, "This is God's camp!" So he named the place Mahanaim.

JACOB SENDS GIFTS TO ESAU

³ Then Jacob sent messengers ahead to his brother, Esau, who was living in the region of Seir in the land of Edom. ⁴ He told them, "Give this message to my master Esau: 'Humble greetings from your servant Jacob. Until now I have been living with Uncle Laban, ⁵ and now I own cattle, donkeys, flocks of sheep and goats, and many servants, both men and women. I have sent these messengers to inform my lord of my coming, hoping that you will be friendly to me.'" ⁶ After delivering the message, the messengers returned to Jacob and reported, "We met your brother, Esau, and he is already on his way to meet you—with an army of 400 men!" ⁷ Jacob was terrified at the news. He divided his household, along with the flocks and herds and camels, into two groups. ⁸ He thought, "If Esau meets one group and attacks it, perhaps the other group can escape." ⁹ Then Jacob prayed, "O God of my grandfather Abraham, and God of my father, Isaac—O Lord, you told me, 'Return to your own land and to your relatives.' And you promised me, 'I will treat you kindly.' ¹⁰ I am not worthy of all the unfailing love and faithfulness you have shown to me, your servant. When I left home and crossed the Jordan River, I owned nothing except a walking stick. Now my household fills two large camps! ¹¹

O Lord, please rescue me from the hand of my brother, Esau. I am afraid that he is coming to attack me, along with my wives and children. ¹² But you promised me, 'I will surely treat you kindly, and I will multiply your descendants until they become as numerous as the sands along the seashore—too many to count.'" ¹³ Jacob stayed where he was for the night. Then he selected these gifts from his possessions to present to his brother, Esau: ¹⁴ 200 female goats, 20 male goats, 200 ewes, 20 rams, ¹⁵ 30 female camels with their young, 40 cows, 10 bulls, 20 female donkeys, and 10 male donkeys. ¹⁶ He divided these animals into herds and assigned each to different servants. Then he told his servants, "Go ahead of me with the animals, but keep some distance between the herds." ¹⁷ He gave these instructions to the men leading the first group: "When my brother, Esau, meets you, he will ask, 'Whose servants are you? Where are you going? Who owns these animals?' ¹⁸ You must reply, 'They belong to your servant Jacob, but they are a gift for his master Esau. Look, he is coming right behind us.'" ¹⁹ Jacob gave the same instructions to the second and third herdsmen and to all who followed behind the herds: "You must say the same thing to Esau when you meet him. ²⁰ And be sure to say, 'Look, your servant Jacob is right behind us.'" Jacob thought, "I will try to appease him by sending gifts ahead of me. When I see him in person, perhaps he will be friendly to me." ²¹ So the gifts were sent on ahead, while Jacob himself spent that night in the camp.

CHAPTER 32

JACOB WRESTLES WITH GOD

[22] During the night Jacob got up and took his two wives, his two servant wives, and his eleven sons and crossed the Jabbok River with them. [23] After taking them to the other side, he sent over all his possessions. [24] This left Jacob all alone in the camp, and a man came and wrestled with him until the dawn began to break. [25] When the man saw that he would not win the match, he touched Jacob's hip and wrenched it out of its socket. [26] Then the man said, "Let me go, for the dawn is breaking!" But Jacob said, "I will not let you go unless you bless me." [27] "What is your name?" the man asked. He replied, "Jacob." [28] "Your name will no longer be Jacob," the man told him. "From now on you will be called Israel, because you have fought with God and with men and have won." [29] "Please tell me your name," Jacob said. "Why do you want to know my name?" the man replied. Then he blessed Jacob there. [30] Jacob named the place Peniel (which means "face of God"), for he said, "I have seen God face to face, yet my life has been spared." [31] The sun was rising as Jacob left Peniel, and he was limping because of the injury to his hip. [32] (Even today the people of Israel don't eat the tendon near the hip socket because of what happened that night when the man strained the tendon of Jacob's hip.)

33

JACOB AND ESAU MAKE PEACE

[1] Then Jacob looked up and saw Esau coming with his 400 men. So he divided the children among Leah, Rachel, and his two servant wives. [2] He put the servant wives and their children at the front, Leah and her children next, and Rachel and Joseph last. [3] Then Jacob went on ahead. As he approached his brother, he bowed to the ground seven times before him. [4] Then Esau ran to meet him and embraced him, threw his arms around his neck, and kissed him. And they both wept. [5] Then Esau looked at the women and children and asked, "Who are these people with you?" "These are the children God has graciously given to me, your servant," Jacob replied. [6] Then the servant wives came forward with their children and bowed before him. [7] Next came Leah with her children, and they bowed before him. Finally, Joseph and Rachel came forward and bowed before him. [8] "And what were all the flocks and herds I met as I came?" Esau asked. Jacob replied, "They are a gift, my lord, to ensure your friendship." [9] "My brother, I have plenty," Esau answered. "Keep what you have for yourself." [10] But Jacob insisted, "No, if I have found favor with you, please accept this gift from me. And what a relief to see your friendly smile. It is like seeing the face of God! [11] Please take this gift I have brought you, for God has been very gracious to me. I have more than enough." And because Jacob insisted, Esau finally accepted the gift. [12] "Well," Esau said, "let's be going. I will lead the way." [13] But Jacob replied, "You can see, my lord, that some of the children are very young, and the flocks and herds have their young, too. If they are driven too hard, even for one day, all the animals could die. [14] Please, my lord, go ahead of your servant. We will follow slowly, at a pace that is comfortable for the livestock and the children. I will meet you at Seir." [15] "All right," Esau said, "but at least let me assign some of my men to guide and protect you." Jacob responded, "That's not necessary. It's enough that you've received me warmly, my lord!" [16] So Esau turned around and started back to Seir that same day. [17] Jacob, on the other hand, traveled on to Succoth. There he built himself a house and made shelters for his livestock. That is why the place was named Succoth (which means "shelters"). [18] Later, having traveled all the way from Paddan-aram, Jacob arrived safely at the town of Shechem, in the land of Canaan. There he set up camp outside the town. [19] Jacob bought the plot of land where he camped from the family of Hamor, the father of Shechem, for 100 pieces of silver. [20] And there he built an altar and named it El-Elohe-Israel.

34

REVENGE AGAINST SHECHEM

¹ One day Dinah, the daughter of Jacob and Leah, went to visit some of the young women who lived in the area. ² But when the local prince, Shechem son of Hamor the Hivite, saw Dinah, he seized her and raped her. ³ But then he fell in love with her, and he tried to win her affection with tender words. ⁴ He said to his father, Hamor, "Get me this young girl. I want to marry her." ⁵ Soon Jacob heard that Shechem had defiled his daughter, Dinah. But since his sons were out in the fields herding his livestock, he said nothing until they returned. ⁶ Hamor, Shechem's father, came to discuss the matter with Jacob. ⁷ Meanwhile, Jacob's sons had come in from the field as soon as they heard what had happened. They were shocked and furious that their sister had been raped. Shechem had done a disgraceful thing against Jacob's family, something that should never be done. ⁸ Hamor tried to speak with Jacob and his sons. "My son Shechem is truly in love with your daughter," he said. "Please let him marry her. ⁹ In fact, let's arrange other marriages, too. You give us your daughters for our sons, and we will give you our daughters for your sons. ¹⁰ And you may live among us; the land is open to you! Settle here and trade with us. And feel free to buy property in the area." ¹¹ Then Shechem himself spoke to Dinah's father and brothers. "Please be kind to me, and let me marry her," he begged. "I will give you whatever you ask. ¹² No matter what dowry or gift you demand, I will gladly pay it—just give me the girl as my wife." ¹³ But since Shechem had defiled their sister, Dinah, Jacob's sons responded deceitfully to Shechem and his father, Hamor. ¹⁴ They said to them, "We couldn't possibly allow this, because you're not circumcised. It would be a disgrace for our sister to marry a man like you! ¹⁵ But here is a solution. If every man among you will be circumcised like we are, ¹⁶ then we will give you our daughters, and we'll take your daughters for ourselves. We will live among you and become one people. ¹⁷ But if you don't agree to be circumcised, we

will take her and be on our way." ¹⁸ Hamor and his son Shechem agreed to their proposal. ¹⁹ Shechem wasted no time in acting on this request, for he wanted Jacob's daughter desperately. Shechem was a highly respected member of his family, ²⁰ and he went with his father, Hamor, to present this proposal to the leaders at the town gate. ²¹ "These men are our friends," they said. "Let's invite them to live here among us and trade freely. Look, the land is large enough to hold them. We can take their daughters as wives and let them marry ours. ²² But they will consider staying here and becoming one people with us only if all of our men are circumcised, just as they are. ²³ But if we do this, all their livestock and possessions will eventually be ours. Come, let's agree to their terms and let them settle here among us." ²⁴ So all the men in the town council agreed with Hamor and Shechem, and every male in the town was circumcised. ²⁵ But three days later, when their wounds were still sore, two of Jacob's sons, Simeon and Levi, who were Dinah's full brothers, took their swords and entered the town without opposition. Then they slaughtered every male there, ²⁶ including Hamor and his son Shechem. They killed them with their swords, then took Dinah from Shechem's house and returned to their camp. ²⁷ Meanwhile, the rest of Jacob's sons arrived. Finding the men slaughtered, they plundered the town because their sister had been defiled there. ²⁸ They seized all the flocks and herds and donkeys—everything they could lay their hands on, both inside the town and outside in the fields. ²⁹ They looted all their wealth and plundered their houses. They also took all their little children and wives and led them away as captives. ³⁰ Afterward Jacob said to Simeon and Levi, "You have ruined me! You've made me stink among all the people of this land—among all the Canaanites and Perizzites. We are so few that they will join forces and crush us. I will be ruined, and my entire household will be wiped out!" ³¹ "But why should we let him treat our sister like a prostitute?" they retorted angrily.

35

JACOB'S RETURN TO BETHEL

[1] Then God said to Jacob, "Get ready and move to Bethel and settle there. Build an altar there to the God who appeared to you when you fled from your brother, Esau." [2] So Jacob told everyone in his household, "Get rid of all your pagan idols, purify yourselves, and put on clean clothing. [3] We are now going to Bethel, where I will build an altar to the God who answered my prayers when I was in distress. He has been with me wherever I have gone." [4] So they gave Jacob all their pagan idols and earrings, and he buried them under the great tree near Shechem. [5] As they set out, a terror from God spread over the people in all the towns of that area, so no one attacked Jacob's family. [6] Eventually, Jacob and his household arrived at Luz (also called Bethel) in Canaan. [7] Jacob built an altar there and named the place El-bethel (which means "God of Bethel"), because God had appeared to him there when he was fleeing from his brother, Esau. [8] Soon after this, Rebekah's old nurse, Deborah, died. She was buried beneath the oak tree in the valley below Bethel. Ever since, the tree has been called Allon-bacuth (which means "oak of weeping"). [9] Now that Jacob had returned from Paddan-aram, God appeared to him again at Bethel. God blessed him, [10] saying, "Your name is Jacob, but you will not be called Jacob any longer. From now on your name will be Israel." So God renamed him Israel. [11] Then God said, "I am El-Shaddai—'God Almighty.' Be fruitful and multiply. You will become a great nation, even many nations. Kings will be among your descendants! [12] And I will give you the land I once gave to Abraham and Isaac. Yes, I will give it to you and your descendants after you." [13] Then God went up from the place where he had spoken to Jacob. [14] Jacob set up a stone pillar to mark the place where God had spoken to him. Then he poured wine over it as an offering to God and anointed the pillar with olive oil. [15] And Jacob named the place Bethel (which means "house of God"), because God had spoken to him there.

THE DEATHS OF RACHEL AND ISAAC

[16] Leaving Bethel, Jacob and his clan moved on toward Ephrath. But Rachel went into labor while they were still some distance away. Her labor pains were intense. [17] After a very hard delivery, the midwife finally exclaimed, "Don't be afraid—you have another son!" [18] Rachel was about to die, but with her last breath she named the baby Ben-oni (which means "son of my sorrow"). The baby's father, however, called him Benjamin (which means "son of my right hand"). [19] So Rachel died and was buried on the way to Ephrath (that is, Bethlehem). [20] Jacob set up a stone monument over Rachel's grave, and it can be seen there to this day. [21] Then Jacob traveled on and camped beyond Migdal-eder. [22] While he was living there, Reuben had intercourse with Bilhah, his father's concubine, and Jacob soon heard about it. These are the names of the twelve sons of Jacob: [23] The sons of Leah were Reuben (Jacob's oldest son), Simeon, Levi, Judah, Issachar, and Zebulun. [24] The sons of Rachel were Joseph and Benjamin. [25] The sons of Bilhah, Rachel's servant, were Dan and Naphtali. [26] The sons of Zilpah, Leah's servant, were Gad and Asher. These are the names of the sons who were born to Jacob at Paddan-aram. [27] So Jacob returned to his father, Isaac, in Mamre, which is near Kiriath-arba (now called Hebron), where Abraham and Isaac had both lived as foreigners. [28] Isaac lived for 180 years. [29] Then he breathed his last and died at a ripe old age, joining his ancestors in death. And his sons, Esau and Jacob, buried him.

CHAPTER 35

36

DESCENDANTS OF ESAU

[1] This is the account of the descendants of Esau (also known as Edom). [2] Esau married two young women from Canaan: Adah, the daughter of Elon the Hittite; and Oholibamah, the daughter of Anah and granddaughter of Zibeon the Hivite. [3] He also married his cousin Basemath, who was the daughter of Ishmael and the sister of Nebaioth. [4] Adah gave birth to a son named Eliphaz for Esau. Basemath gave birth to a son named Reuel. [5] Oholibamah gave birth to sons named Jeush, Jalam, and Korah. All these sons were born to Esau in the land of Canaan. [6] Esau took his wives, his children, and his entire household, along with his livestock and cattle—all the wealth he had acquired in the land of Canaan—and moved away from his brother, Jacob. [7] There was not enough land to support them both because of all the livestock and possessions they had acquired. [8] So Esau (also known as Edom) settled in the hill country of Seir. [9] This is the account of Esau's descendants, the Edomites, who lived in the hill country of Seir. [10] These are the names of Esau's sons: Eliphaz, the son of Esau's wife Adah; and Reuel, the son of Esau's wife Basemath. [11] The descendants of Eliphaz were Teman, Omar, Zepho, Gatam, and

Kenaz. ¹²Timna, the concubine of Esau's son Eliphaz, gave birth to a son named Amalek. These are the descendants of Esau's wife Adah. ¹³ The descendants of Reuel were Nahath, Zerah, Shammah, and Mizzah. These are the descendants of Esau's wife Basemath. ¹⁴ Esau also had sons through Oholibamah, the daughter of Anah and granddaughter of Zibeon. Their names were Jeush, Jalam, and Korah. ¹⁵ These are the descendants of Esau who became the leaders of various clans: The descendants of Esau's oldest son, Eliphaz, became the leaders of the clans of Teman, Omar, Zepho, Kenaz, ¹⁶ Korah, Gatam, and Amalek. These are the clan leaders in the land of Edom who descended from Eliphaz. All these were descendants of Esau's wife Adah. ¹⁷ The descendants of Esau's son Reuel became the leaders of the clans of Nahath, Zerah, Shammah, and Mizzah. These are the clan leaders in the land of Edom who descended from Reuel. All these were descendants of Esau's wife Basemath. ¹⁸ The descendants of Esau and his wife Oholibamah became the leaders of the clans of Jeush, Jalam, and Korah. These are the clan leaders who descended from Esau's wife Oholibamah, the daughter of Anah. ¹⁹ These are the clans descended from Esau (also known as Edom), identified by their clan leaders.

ORIGINAL PEOPLES OF EDOM

[20] These are the names of the tribes that descended from Seir the Horite. They lived in the land of Edom: Lotan, Shobal, Zibeon, Anah, [21] Dishon, Ezer, and Dishan. These were the Horite clan leaders, the descendants of Seir, who lived in the land of Edom. [22] The descendants of Lotan were Hori and Hemam. Lotan's sister was named Timna. [23] The descendants of Shobal were Alvan, Manahath, Ebal, Shepho, and Onam. [24] The descendants of Zibeon were Aiah and Anah. (This is the Anah who discovered the hot springs in the wilderness while he was grazing his father's donkeys.) [25] The descendants of Anah were his son, Dishon, and his daughter, Oholibamah. [26] The descendants of Dishon were Hemdan, Eshban, Ithran, and Keran. [27] The descendants of Ezer were Bilhan, Zaavan, and Akan. [28] The descendants of Dishan were Uz and Aran. [29] So these were the leaders of the Horite clans: Lotan, Shobal, Zibeon, Anah, [30] Dishon, Ezer, and Dishan. The Horite clans are named after their clan leaders, who lived in the land of Seir.

RULERS OF EDOM

[31] These are the kings who ruled in the land of Edom before any king ruled over the Israelites: [32] Bela son of Beor, who ruled in Edom from his city of Dinhabah. [33] When Bela died, Jobab son of Zerah from Bozrah became king in his place. [34] When Jobab died, Husham from the land of the Temanites became king in his place. [35] When Husham died, Hadad son of Bedad became king in his place and ruled from the city of Avith. He was the one who defeated the Midianites in the land of Moab. [36] When Hadad died, Samlah from the city of Masrekah became king in his place. [37] When Samlah died, Shaul from the city of Rehoboth-on-the-River became king in his place. [38] When Shaul died, Baal-hanan son of Acbor became king in his place. [39] When Baal-hanan son of Acbor died, Hadad became king in his place and ruled from the city of Pau. His wife was Mehetabel, the daughter of Matred and granddaughter of Me-zahab. [40] These are the names of the leaders of the clans descended from Esau, who lived in the places named for them: Timna, Alvah, Jetheth, [41] Oholibamah, Elah, Pinon, [42] Kenaz, Teman, Mibzar, [43] Magdiel, and Iram. These are the leaders of the clans of Edom, listed according to their settlements in the land they occupied. They all descended from Esau, the ancestor of the Edomites.

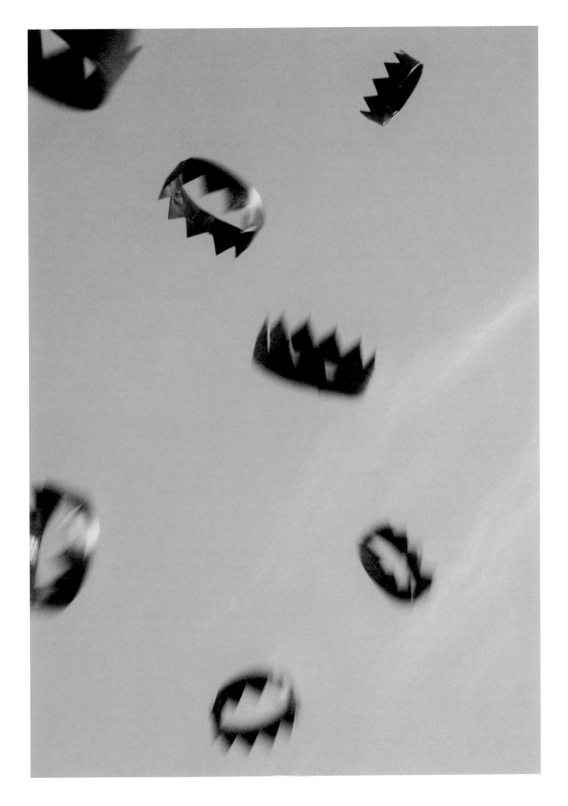

CHAPTER 36

37

JOSEPH'S DREAMS

[1] So Jacob settled again in the land of Canaan, where his father had lived as a foreigner. [2] This is the account of Jacob and his family. When Joseph was seventeen years old, he often tended his father's flocks. He worked for his half brothers, the sons of his father's wives Bilhah and Zilpah. But Joseph reported to his father some of the bad things his brothers were doing. [3] Jacob loved Joseph more than any of his other children because Joseph had been born to him in his old age. So one day Jacob had a special gift made for Joseph—a beautiful robe. [4] But his brothers hated Joseph because their father loved him more than the rest of them. They couldn't say a kind word to him. [5] One night Joseph had a dream, and when he told his brothers about it, they hated him more than ever. [6] "Listen to this dream," he said. [7] "We were out in the field, tying up bundles of grain. Suddenly my bundle stood up, and your bundles all gathered around and bowed low before mine!" [8] His brothers responded, "So you think you will be our king, do you? Do you actually think you will reign over us?" And they hated him all the more because of his dreams and the way he talked about them. [9] Soon Joseph had another dream, and again he told his brothers about it. "Listen, I have had another dream," he said. "The sun, moon, and eleven stars bowed low before me!" [10] This time he told the dream to his father as well as to his brothers, but his father scolded him. "What kind of dream is that?" he asked. "Will your mother and I and your brothers actually come and bow to the ground before you?" [11] But while his brothers were jealous of Joseph, his father wondered what the dreams meant. [12] Soon after this, Joseph's brothers went to pasture their father's flocks at Shechem. [13] When they had been gone for some time, Jacob said to Joseph, "Your brothers are pasturing the sheep at Shechem. Get ready, and I will send you to them." "I'm ready to go," Joseph replied. [14] "Go and see how your brothers and the flocks are getting along," Jacob said. "Then come back and bring me a report." So Jacob sent him on his way, and Joseph traveled to Shechem from their home in the valley of Hebron. [15] When he arrived there, a man from the area noticed him wandering around the countryside. "What are you looking for?" he asked. [16] "I'm looking for my brothers," Joseph replied. "Do you know where they are pasturing their sheep?" [17] "Yes," the man told him. "They have moved on from here, but I heard them say, 'Let's go on to Dothan.'" So Joseph followed his brothers to Dothan and found them there.

JOSEPH SOLD INTO SLAVERY

[18] When Joseph's brothers saw him coming, they recognized him in the distance. As he approached, they made plans to kill him. [19] "Here comes the dreamer!" they said. [20] "Come on, let's kill him and throw him into one of these cisterns. We can tell our father, 'A wild animal has eaten him.' Then we'll see what becomes of his dreams!" [21] But when Reuben heard of their scheme, he came to Joseph's rescue. "Let's not kill him," he said. [22] "Why should we shed any blood? Let's just throw him into this empty cistern here in the wilderness. Then he'll die without our laying a hand on him." Reuben was secretly planning to rescue Joseph and return him to his father. [23] So when Joseph arrived, his brothers ripped off the beautiful robe he was wearing. [24] Then they grabbed him and threw him into the cistern. Now the cistern was empty; there was no water in it. [25] Then, just as they were sitting down to eat, they looked up and saw a caravan of camels in the distance coming toward them. It was a group of Ishmaelite traders taking a load of gum, balm, and aromatic resin from Gilead down to Egypt. [26] Judah said to his brothers, "What will we gain by killing our brother? We'd have to cover up the crime. [27] Instead of hurting him, let's sell him to those Ishmaelite traders. After all, he is our brother—our own flesh and blood!" And his brothers agreed. [28] So when the Ishmaelites, who were Midianite traders, came by, Joseph's brothers pulled him out of the cistern and sold him to them for twenty pieces of silver. And the traders took him to Egypt. [29] Some time later, Reuben returned to get Joseph out of the cistern. When he discovered that Joseph was missing, he tore his clothes in grief. [30] Then he went back to his brothers and lamented, "The boy is gone! What will I do now?" [31] Then the brothers killed a young goat and dipped Joseph's robe in its blood. [32] They sent the beautiful robe to their father with this message: "Look at what we found. Doesn't this robe belong to your son?" [33] Their father recognized it immediately. "Yes," he said, "it is my son's robe. A wild animal must have eaten him. Joseph has clearly been torn to pieces!" [34] Then Jacob tore his clothes and dressed himself in burlap. He mourned deeply for his son for a long time. [35] His family all tried to comfort him, but he refused to be comforted. "I will go to my grave mourning for my son," he would say, and then he would weep. [36] Meanwhile, the Midianite traders arrived in Egypt, where they sold Joseph to Potiphar, an officer of Pharaoh, the king of Egypt. Potiphar was captain of the palace guard.

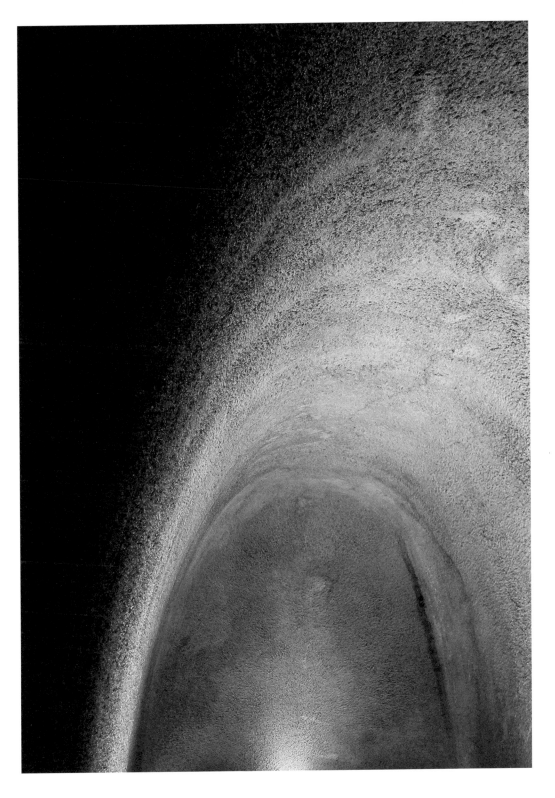

JUDAH AND TAMAR

[1] About this time, Judah left home and moved to Adullam, where he stayed with a man named Hirah. [2] There he saw a Canaanite woman, the daughter of Shua, and he married her. When he slept with her, [3] she became pregnant and gave birth to a son, and he named the boy Er. [4] Then she became pregnant again and gave birth to another son, and she named him Onan. [5] And when she gave birth to a third son, she named him Shelah. At the time of Shelah's birth, they were living at Kezib. [6] In the course of time, Judah arranged for his firstborn son, Er, to marry a young woman named Tamar. [7] But Er was a wicked man in the Lord's sight, so the Lord took his life. [8] Then Judah said to Er's brother Onan, "Go and marry Tamar, as our law requires of the brother of a man who has died. You must produce an heir for your brother." [9] But Onan was not willing to have a child who would not be his own heir. So whenever he had intercourse with his brother's wife, he spilled the semen on the ground. This prevented her from having a child who would belong to his brother. [10] But the Lord considered it evil for Onan to deny a child to his dead brother. So the Lord took Onan's life, too. [11] Then Judah said to Tamar, his daughter-in-law, "Go back to your parents' home and remain a widow until my son Shelah is old enough to marry you." (But Judah didn't really intend to do this because he was afraid Shelah would also die, like his two brothers.) So Tamar went back to live in her father's home. [12] Some years later Judah's wife died. After the time of mourning was over, Judah and his friend Hirah the Adullamite went up to Timnah to supervise the shearing of his sheep. [13] Someone told Tamar, "Look, your father-in-law is going up to Timnah to shear his sheep." [14] Tamar was aware that Shelah had grown up, but no arrangements had been made for her to come and marry him. So she changed out of her widow's clothing and covered herself with a veil to disguise herself. Then she sat beside the road at the entrance to the village of Enaim, which is on the road to Timnah. [15] Judah noticed her and thought she was a prostitute, since she had covered her face. [16] So he stopped and propositioned her. "Let me have sex with you," he said, not realizing that she was his own daughter-in-law. "How much

will you pay to have sex with me?" Tamar asked. [17] "I'll send you a young goat from my flock," Judah promised. "But what will you give me to guarantee that you will send the goat?" she asked. [18] "What kind of guarantee do you want?" he replied. She answered, "Leave me your identification seal and its cord and the walking stick you are carrying." So Judah gave them to her. Then he had intercourse with her, and she became pregnant. [19] Afterward she went back home, took off her veil, and put on her widow's clothing as usual. [20] Later Judah asked his friend Hirah the Adullamite to take the young goat to the woman and to pick up the things he had given her as his guarantee. But Hirah couldn't find her. [21] So he asked the men who lived there, "Where can I find the shrine prostitute who was sitting beside the road at the entrance to Enaim?" "We've never had a shrine prostitute here," they replied. [22] So Hirah returned to Judah and told him, "I couldn't find her anywhere, and the men of the village claim they've never had a shrine prostitute there." [23] "Then let her keep the things I gave her," Judah said. "I sent the young goat as we agreed, but you couldn't find her. We'd be the

laughingstock of the village if we went back again to look for her." [24] About three months later, Judah was told, "Tamar, your daughter-in-law, has acted like a prostitute. And now, because of this, she's pregnant." "Bring her out, and let her be burned!" Judah demanded. [25] But as they were taking her out to kill her, she sent this message to her father-in-law: "The man who owns these things made me pregnant. Look closely. Whose seal and cord and walking stick are these?" [26] Judah recognized them immediately and said, "She is more righteous than I am, because I didn't arrange for her to marry my son Shelah." And Judah never slept with Tamar again. [27] When the time came for Tamar to give birth, it was discovered that she was carrying twins. [28] While she was in labor, one of the babies reached out his hand. The midwife grabbed it and tied a scarlet string around the child's wrist, announcing, "This one came out first." [29] But then he pulled back his hand, and out came his brother! "What!" the midwife exclaimed. "How did you break out first?" So he was named Perez. [30] Then the baby with the scarlet string on his wrist was born, and he was named Zerah.

39

JOSEPH IN POTIPHAR'S HOUSE

[1] When Joseph was taken to Egypt by the Ishmaelite traders, he was purchased by Potiphar, an Egyptian officer. Potiphar was captain of the guard for Pharaoh, the king of Egypt. [2] The Lord was with Joseph, so he succeeded in everything he did as he served in the home of his Egyptian master. [3] Potiphar noticed this and realized that the Lord was with Joseph, giving him success in everything he did. [4] This pleased Potiphar, so he soon made Joseph his personal attendant. He put him in charge of his entire household and everything he owned. [5] From the day Joseph was put in charge of his master's household and property, the Lord began to bless Potiphar's household for Joseph's sake. All his household affairs ran smoothly, and his crops and livestock flourished. [6] So Potiphar gave Joseph complete administrative responsibility over everything he owned. With Joseph there, he didn't worry about a thing—except what kind of food to eat! Joseph was a very handsome

and well-built young man, [7] and Potiphar's wife soon began to look at him lustfully. "Come and sleep with me," she demanded. [8] But Joseph refused. "Look," he told her, "my master trusts me with everything in his entire household. [9] No one here has more authority than I do. He has held back nothing from me except you, because you are his wife. How could I do such a wicked thing? It would be a great sin against God." [10] She kept putting pressure on Joseph day after day, but he refused to sleep with her, and he kept out of her way as much as possible. [11] One day, however, no one else was around when he went in to do his work. [12] She came and grabbed him by his cloak, demanding, "Come on, sleep with me!" Joseph tore himself away, but he left his cloak in her hand as he ran from the house. [13] When she saw that she was holding his cloak and he had fled, [14] she called out to her servants. Soon all the men came running. "Look!" she said. "My husband has brought this Hebrew slave here to make fools of us! He came into my room to rape me, but I screamed. [15] When he heard me scream, he ran outside and got away, but he left his cloak behind with me." [16] She kept the cloak with her until her husband came home. [17] Then she told him her story. "That Hebrew slave you've brought into our house tried to come in and fool around with me," she said. [18] "But when I screamed, he ran outside, leaving his cloak with me!"

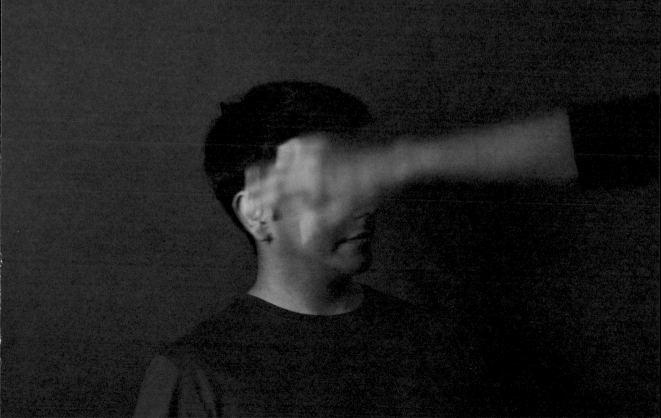

JOSEPH PUT IN PRISON

[19] Potiphar was furious when he heard his wife's story about how Joseph had treated her. [20] So he took Joseph and threw him into the prison where the king's prisoners were held, and there he remained. [21] But the Lord was with Joseph in the prison and showed him his faithful love. And the Lord made Joseph a favorite with the

prison warden. [22] Before long, the warden put Joseph in charge of all the other prisoners and over everything that happened in the prison. [23] The warden had no more worries, because Joseph took care of everything. The Lord was with him and caused everything he did to succeed.

40

JOSEPH INTERPRETS TWO DREAMS

[1] Some time later, Pharaoh's chief cup-bearer and chief baker offended their royal master. [2] Pharaoh became angry with these two officials, [3] and he put them in the prison where Joseph was, in the palace of the captain of the guard. [4] They remained in prison for quite some time, and the captain of the guard assigned them to Joseph, who looked after them. [5] While they were in prison, Pharaoh's cup-bearer and baker each had a dream one night, and each dream had its own meaning. [6] When Joseph saw them the next morning, he noticed that they both looked upset. [7] "Why do you look so worried today?" he asked them. [8] And they replied, "We both had dreams last night, but no one can tell us what they mean." "Interpreting dreams is God's business," Joseph replied. "Go ahead and tell me your dreams." [9] So the chief cup-bearer told Joseph his dream first. "In my dream," he said, "I saw a grapevine in front of me. [10] The vine had three branches that began to bud and blossom, and soon it produced clusters of ripe grapes. [11] I was holding Pharaoh's wine cup in my hand, so I took a cluster of grapes and squeezed the juice into the cup. Then I placed the cup in Pharaoh's hand." [12] "This is what the dream means," Joseph said. "The three branches represent three days. [13] Within three days Pharaoh will lift you up and restore you to your position as his chief

cup-bearer. [14] And please remember me and do me a favor when things go well for you. Mention me to Pharaoh, so he might let me out of this place. [15] For I was kidnapped from my homeland, the land of the Hebrews, and now I'm here in prison, but I did nothing to deserve it." [16] When the chief baker saw that Joseph had given the first dream such a positive interpretation, he said to Joseph, "I had a dream, too. In my dream there were three baskets of white pastries stacked on my head. [17] The top basket contained all kinds of pastries for Pharaoh, but the birds came and ate them from the basket on my head." [18] "This is what the dream means," Joseph told him. "The three baskets also represent three days. [19] Three days from now Pharaoh will lift you up and impale your body on a pole. Then birds will come and peck away at your flesh." [20] Pharaoh's birthday came three days later, and he prepared a banquet for all his officials and staff. He summoned his chief cup-bearer and chief baker to join the other officials. [21] He then restored the chief cup-bearer to his former position, so he could again hand Pharaoh his cup. [22] But Pharaoh impaled the chief baker, just as Joseph had predicted when he interpreted his dream. [23] Pharaoh's chief cup-bearer, however, forgot all about Joseph, never giving him another thought.

41

PHARAOH'S DREAMS

[1] Two full years later, Pharaoh dreamed that he was standing on the bank of the Nile River. [2] In his dream he saw seven fat, healthy cows come up out of the river and begin grazing in the marsh grass. [3] Then he saw seven more cows come up behind them from the Nile, but these were scrawny and thin. These cows stood beside the fat cows on the riverbank. [4] Then the scrawny, thin cows ate the seven healthy, fat cows! At this point in the dream, Pharaoh woke up. [5] But he fell asleep again and had a second dream. This time he saw seven heads of grain, plump and beautiful, growing on a single stalk. [6] Then seven more heads of grain appeared, but these were shriveled and withered by the east wind. [7] And these thin heads swallowed up the seven plump, well-formed heads! Then Pharaoh woke up again and realized it was a dream. [8] The next morning Pharaoh was very disturbed by the dreams. So he called for all the magicians and wise men of Egypt. When Pharaoh told them his dreams, not one of them could tell him what they meant. [9] Finally, the king's chief cup-bearer spoke up. "Today I have been reminded of my failure," he told Pharaoh. [10] "Some time ago, you were angry with the chief baker and me, and you imprisoned us in the palace of the captain of the guard. [11] One night the chief baker and I each had a dream, and each dream had its own meaning. [12] There was a young Hebrew man with us in the prison who was a slave of the captain of the guard. We told him our dreams, and he told us what each of our dreams meant. [13] And everything happened just as he had predicted. I was restored to my position as cup-bearer, and the chief baker was executed and impaled on a pole." [14] Pharaoh sent for Joseph at once, and he was quickly brought from the prison. After he shaved and changed his clothes, he went in and stood before Pharaoh. [15] Then Pharaoh said to Joseph, "I had a dream last night, and no one here can tell me what it means. But I have heard that when you hear about a dream you can interpret it." [16] "It is beyond my power to do this," Joseph replied. "But God can tell you what it means and set you at ease." [17] So Pharaoh told Joseph his dream. "In my dream," he said, "I was standing on the bank of the Nile River, [18] and I saw seven fat, healthy cows come up out of the river and begin grazing in the marsh grass. [19] But then I saw seven sick-looking cows, scrawny and thin, come up after them. I've never seen such sorry-looking animals in all the land of Egypt. [20] These thin, scrawny cows ate the seven fat cows.

^{21} But afterward you wouldn't have known it, for they were still as thin and scrawny as before! Then I woke up. ^{22} "In my dream I also saw seven heads of grain, full and beautiful, growing on a single stalk. ^{23} Then seven more heads of grain appeared, but these were blighted, shriveled, and withered by the east wind. ^{24} And the shriveled heads swallowed the seven healthy heads. I told these dreams to the magicians, but no one could tell me what they mean." ^{25} Joseph responded, "Both of Pharaoh's dreams mean the same thing. God is telling Pharaoh in advance what he is about to do. ^{26} The seven healthy cows and the seven healthy heads of grain both represent seven years of prosperity. ^{27} The seven thin, scrawny cows that came up later and the seven thin heads of grain, withered by the east wind, represent seven years of famine. ^{28} This will happen just as I have described it, for God has revealed to Pharaoh in advance what he is about to do. ^{29} The next seven years will be a period of great prosperity throughout the land of Egypt. [30] But afterward there will be seven years of famine so great that all the prosperity will be forgotten in Egypt. Famine will destroy the land. [31] This famine will be so severe that even the memory of the good years will be erased. [32] As for having two similar dreams, it means that these events have been decreed by God, and he will soon make them happen. [33] Therefore, Pharaoh should find an intelligent and wise man and put him in charge of the entire land of Egypt. [34] Then Pharaoh should appoint supervisors over the land and let them collect one-fifth of all the crops during the seven good years. [35] Have them gather all the food produced in the good years that are just ahead and bring it to Pharaoh's storehouses. Store it away, and guard it so there will be food in the cities. [36] That way there will be enough to eat when the seven years of famine come to the land of Egypt. Otherwise this famine will destroy the land."

JOSEPH MADE RULER OF EGYPT

[37] Joseph's suggestions were well received by Pharaoh and his officials. [38] So Pharaoh asked his officials, "Can we find anyone else like this man so obviously filled with the spirit of God?" [39] Then Pharaoh said to Joseph, "Since God has revealed the meaning of the dreams to you, clearly no one else is as intelligent or wise as you are. [40] You will be in charge of my court, and all my people will take orders from you. Only I, sitting on my throne, will have a rank higher than yours." [41] Pharaoh said to Joseph, "I hereby put you in charge of the entire land of Egypt." [42] Then Pharaoh removed his signet ring from his hand and placed it on Joseph's finger. He dressed him in fine linen clothing and hung a gold chain around his neck. [43] Then he had Joseph ride in the chariot reserved for his second-in-command. And wherever Joseph went, the command was shouted, "Kneel down!" So Pharaoh put Joseph in charge of all Egypt. [44] And Pharaoh said to him, "I am Pharaoh, but no one will lift a hand or foot in the entire land of Egypt without your approval." [45] Then Pharaoh gave Joseph a new Egyptian name, Zaphenath-paneah. He also gave him a wife, whose name was Asenath. She was the daughter of Potiphera, the priest of On. So Joseph took charge of the entire land of Egypt. [46] He was thirty years old when he began serving in the court of Pharaoh, the king of Egypt. And when Joseph left Pharaoh's presence, he inspected the entire land of Egypt. [47] As predicted, for seven years the land produced bumper crops. [48] During those years, Joseph gathered all the crops grown in Egypt and stored the grain from the surrounding fields in the cities. [49] He piled up huge amounts of grain like sand on the seashore. Finally, he stopped keeping records because there was too much to measure. [50] During this time, before the first of the famine years, two sons were born to Joseph and his wife, Asenath, the daughter of Potiphera, the priest of On. [51] Joseph named his older son Manasseh, for he said, "God has made me forget all my troubles and everyone in my father's family." [52] Joseph named his second son Ephraim, for he said, "God has made me fruitful in this land of my grief." [53] At last the seven years of bumper crops throughout the land of Egypt came to an end. [54] Then the seven years of famine began, just as Joseph had predicted. The famine also struck all the surrounding countries, but throughout Egypt there was plenty of food. [55] Eventually, however, the famine spread throughout the land of Egypt as well. And when the people cried out to Pharaoh for food, he told them, "Go to Joseph, and do whatever he tells you." [56] So with severe famine everywhere, Joseph opened up the storehouses and distributed grain to the Egyptians, for the famine was severe throughout the land of Egypt. [57] And people from all around came to Egypt to buy grain from Joseph because the famine was severe throughout the world.

42

JOSEPH'S BROTHERS GO TO EGYPT

[1] When Jacob heard that grain was available in Egypt, he said to his sons, "Why are you standing around looking at one another? [2] I have heard there is grain in Egypt. Go down there, and buy enough grain to keep us alive. Otherwise we'll die." [3] So Joseph's ten older brothers went down to Egypt to buy grain. [4] But Jacob wouldn't let Joseph's younger brother, Benjamin, go with them, for fear some harm might come to him. [5] So Jacob's sons arrived in Egypt along with others to buy food, for the famine was in Canaan as well. [6] Since Joseph was governor of all Egypt and in charge of selling grain to all the people, it was to him that his brothers came. When they arrived, they bowed before him with their faces to the ground. [7] Joseph recognized his brothers instantly, but he pretended to be a stranger and spoke harshly to them. "Where are you from?" he demanded. "From the land of Canaan," they replied. "We have come to buy food." [8] Although Joseph recognized his brothers, they didn't recognize him. [9] And he remembered the dreams he'd had about them many years before. He said to them, "You are spies! You have come to see how vulnerable our land has become." [10] "No, my lord!" they exclaimed. "Your servants have simply come to buy food. [11] We are all brothers—members of the same family. We are honest men, sir! We are not spies!" [12] "Yes, you are!" Joseph insisted. "You have come to see how vulnerable our land has become." [13] "Sir," they said, "there are actually twelve of us. We, your servants, are all brothers, sons of a man living in the land of Canaan. Our youngest brother is back there with our father right now, and one of our brothers is no longer with us." [14] But Joseph insisted, "As I said, you are spies! [15] This is how I will test your story. I swear by the life of Pharaoh that you will never leave Egypt unless your youngest brother comes here! [16] One of you must go and get your brother. I'll keep the rest of you here in prison. Then we'll find out whether or not your story is true. By the life of Pharaoh, if it turns out that you don't have a younger brother, then I'll know you are spies." [17] So Joseph put them all in prison for three days. [18] On the third day Joseph said to them, "I am a God-fearing man. If you do as I say, you will live. [19] If you really are honest men, choose one of your brothers to remain in prison. The rest of you may go home with grain for your starving families. [20] But you must bring your youngest brother back to me. This will prove that you are telling the truth, and you will not die." To this they agreed. [21] Speaking among themselves, they said, "Clearly we are being punished because of what we did to Joseph long ago. We saw his anguish when he pleaded for his life, but we wouldn't listen. That's why we're in this trouble." [22] "Didn't I tell you not to sin against the boy?" Reuben asked. "But you wouldn't listen. And now we have to answer for his blood!" [23] Of course, they didn't know that Joseph understood them, for he had been speaking to them through an interpreter.

²⁴ Now he turned away from them and began to weep. When he regained his composure, he spoke to them again. Then he chose Simeon from among them and had him tied up right before their eyes. ²⁵ Joseph then ordered his servants to fill the men's sacks with grain, but he also gave secret instructions to return each brother's payment at the top of his sack. He also gave them supplies for their journey home. ²⁶ So the brothers loaded their donkeys with the grain and headed for home. ²⁷ But when they stopped for the night and one of them opened his sack to get grain for his donkey, he found his money in the top of his sack. ²⁸ "Look!" he exclaimed to his brothers. "My money has been returned; it's here in my sack!" Then their hearts sank. Trembling, they said to each other, "What has God done to us?" ²⁹ When the brothers came to their father, Jacob, in the land of Canaan, they told him everything that had happened to them. ³⁰ "The man who is governor of the land spoke very harshly to us," they told him. "He accused us of being spies scouting the land. ³¹ But we said, 'We are honest men, not spies. ³² We are twelve brothers, sons of one father. One brother is no longer with us, and the youngest is at home with our father in the land of Canaan.' ³³ Then the man who is governor of the land told us, 'This is how I will find out if you are honest men. Leave one of your brothers here with me, and take grain for your starving families and go on home. ³⁴ But you must bring your youngest brother back to me. Then I will know you are honest men and not spies. Then I will give you back your brother, and you may trade freely in the land.'" ³⁵ As they emptied out their sacks, there in each man's sack was the bag of money he had paid for the grain! The brothers and their father were terrified when they saw the bags of money. ³⁶ Jacob exclaimed, "You are robbing me of my children! Joseph is gone! Simeon is gone! And now you want to take Benjamin, too. Everything is going against me!" ³⁷ Then Reuben said to his father, "You may kill my two sons if I don't bring Benjamin back to you. I'll be responsible for him, and I promise to bring him back." ³⁸ But Jacob replied, "My son will not go down with you. His brother Joseph is dead, and he is all I have left. If anything should happen to him on your journey, you would send this grieving, white-haired man to his grave."

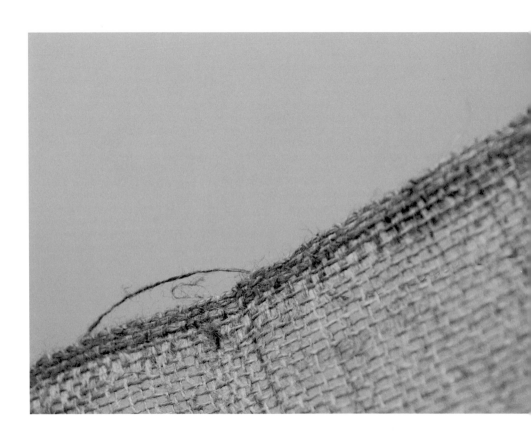

43

THE BROTHERS RETURN TO EGYPT

[1] But the famine continued to ravage the land of Canaan. [2] When the grain they had brought from Egypt was almost gone, Jacob said to his sons, "Go back and buy us a little more food." [3] But Judah said, "The man was serious when he warned us, 'You won't see my face again unless your brother is with you.' [4] If you send Benjamin with us, we will go down and buy more food. [5] But if you don't let Benjamin go, we won't go either. Remember, the man said, 'You won't see my face again unless your brother is with you.'" [6] "Why were you so cruel to me?" Jacob moaned. "Why did you tell him you had another brother?" [7] "The man kept asking us questions about our family," they replied. "He asked, 'Is your father still alive? Do you have another brother?' So we answered his questions. How could we know he would say, 'Bring your brother down here'?" [8] Judah said to his father, "Send the boy with me, and we will be on our way. Otherwise we will all die of starvation—and not only we, but you and our little ones. [9] I personally guarantee his safety. You may hold me responsible if I don't bring him back to you. Then let me bear the blame forever. [10] If we hadn't wasted all this time, we could have gone and returned twice by now." [11] So their father, Jacob, finally said to them, "If it can't be avoided, then at

least do this. Pack your bags with the best products of this land. Take them down to the man as gifts—balm, honey, gum, aromatic resin, pistachio nuts, and almonds. [12] Also take double the money that was put back in your sacks, as it was probably someone's mistake. [13] Then take your brother, and go back to the man. [14] May God Almighty give you mercy as you go before the man, so that he will release Simeon and let Benjamin return. But if I must lose my children, so be it." [15] So the men packed Jacob's gifts and double the money and headed off with Benjamin. They finally arrived in Egypt and presented themselves to Joseph. [16] When Joseph saw Benjamin with them, he said to the manager of his household, "These men will eat with me this noon. Take them inside the palace. Then go slaughter an animal, and prepare a big feast." [17] So the man did as Joseph told him and took them into Joseph's palace. [18] The brothers were terrified when they saw that they were being taken into Joseph's house. "It's because of the money someone put in our sacks last time we were here," they said. "He plans to pretend that we stole it. Then he will seize us, make us slaves, and take our donkeys."

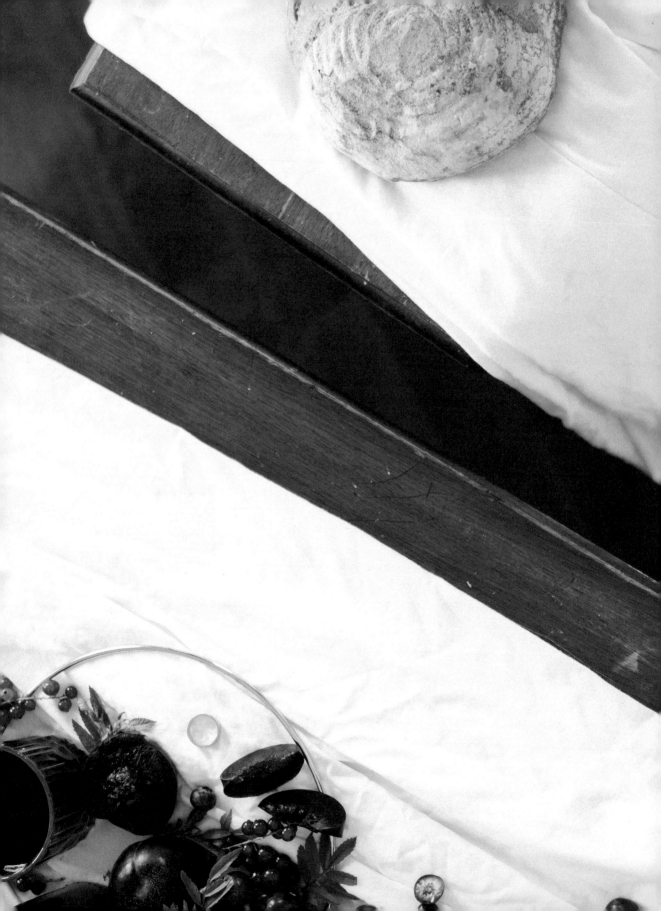

A FEAST AT JOSEPH'S PALACE

[19] The brothers approached the manager of Joseph's household and spoke to him at the entrance to the palace. [20] "Sir," they said, "we came to Egypt once before to buy food. [21] But as we were returning home, we stopped for the night and opened our sacks. Then we discovered that each man's money—the exact amount paid—was in the top of his sack! Here it is; we have brought it back with us. [22] We also have additional money to buy more food. We have no idea who put our money in our sacks." [23] "Relax. Don't be afraid," the household manager told them. "Your God, the God of your father, must have put this treasure into your sacks. I know I received your payment." Then he released Simeon and brought him out to them. [24] The manager then led the men into Joseph's palace. He gave them water to wash their feet and provided food for their donkeys. [25] They were told they would be eating there, so they prepared their gifts for Joseph's arrival at noon. [26] When Joseph came home, they gave him the gifts they had brought him, then bowed low to the ground before him. [27] After greeting them, he asked, "How is your father, the old man you spoke about? Is he still alive?" [28] "Yes," they replied. "Our father, your servant, is alive and well." And they bowed low again. [29] Then Joseph looked at his brother Benjamin, the son of his own mother. "Is this your youngest brother, the one you told me about?" Joseph asked. "May God be gracious to you, my son." [30] Then Joseph hurried from the room because he was overcome with emotion for his brother. He went into his private room, where he broke down and wept. [31] After washing his face, he came back out, keeping himself under control. Then he ordered, "Bring out the food!" [32] The waiters served Joseph at his own table, and his brothers were served at a separate table. The Egyptians who ate with Joseph sat at their own table, because Egyptians despise Hebrews and refuse to eat with them. [33] Joseph told each of his brothers where to sit, and to their amazement, he seated them according to age, from oldest to youngest. [34] And Joseph filled their plates with food from his own table, giving Benjamin five times as much as he gave the others. So they feasted and drank freely with him.

44

JOSEPH'S SILVER CUP

[1] When his brothers were ready to leave, Joseph gave these instructions to his palace manager: "Fill each of their sacks with as much grain as they can carry, and put each man's money back into his sack. [2] Then put my personal silver cup at the top of the youngest brother's sack, along with the money for his grain." So the manager did as Joseph instructed him. [3] The brothers were up at dawn and were sent on their journey with their loaded donkeys. [4] But when they had gone only a short distance and were barely out of the city, Joseph said to his palace manager, "Chase after them and stop them. When you catch up with them, ask them, 'Why have you repaid my kindness with such evil? [5] Why have you stolen my master's silver cup, which he uses to predict the future? What a wicked thing you have done!'" [6] When the palace manager caught up with the men, he spoke to them as he had been instructed. [7] "What are you talking about?" the brothers responded. "We are your servants and would never do such a thing! [8] Didn't we return the money we found in our sacks? We brought it back all the way from the land of Canaan. Why would we steal silver or gold from your master's house? [9] If you find his cup with any one of us, let that man die. And all the rest of us, my lord, will be your slaves." [10] "That's fair," the man replied. "But only the one who stole the cup will be my slave. The rest of you may go free." [11] They all quickly took their sacks from the backs of their donkeys and opened them. [12] The palace manager searched the brothers' sacks, from the oldest to the youngest. And the cup was found in Benjamin's sack! [13] When the brothers saw this, they tore their clothing in despair. Then they loaded their donkeys again and returned to the city. [14] Joseph was still in his palace when Judah and his brothers arrived, and they fell to the ground before him. [15] "What have you done?" Joseph demanded. "Don't you know that a man like me can predict the future?" [16] Judah answered, "Oh, my lord, what can we say to you? How can we explain this? How can we prove our innocence? God is punishing us for our sins. My lord, we have all returned to be your slaves—all of us, not just our brother who had your cup in his sack." [17] "No," Joseph said. "I would never do such a thing! Only the man who stole the cup will be my slave. The rest of you may go back to your father in peace."

JUDAH SPEAKS FOR HIS BROTHERS

[18] Then Judah stepped forward and said, "Please, my lord, let your servant say just one word to you. Please, do not be angry with me, even though you are as powerful as Pharaoh himself. [19] My lord, previously you asked us, your servants, 'Do you have a father or a brother?' [20] And we responded, 'Yes, my lord, we have a father who is an old man, and his youngest son is a child of his old age. His full brother is dead, and he alone is left of his mother's children, and his father loves him very much.' [21] And you said to us, 'Bring him here so I can see him with my own eyes.' [22] But we said to you, 'My lord, the boy cannot leave his father, for his father would die.' [23] But you told us, 'Unless your youngest brother comes with you, you will never see my face again.' [24] So we returned to your servant, our father, and told him what you had said. [25] Later, when he said, 'Go back again and buy us more food,' [26] we replied, 'We can't go unless you let our youngest brother go with us. We'll never get to see the man's face unless our youngest brother is with us.' [27] Then my father said to us, 'As you know, my wife had two sons, [28] and one of them went away and never returned. Doubtless he was torn to pieces by some wild animal. I have never seen him since. [29] Now if you take his brother away from me, and any harm comes to him, you will send this grieving, white-haired man to his grave.' [30] And now, my lord, I cannot go back to my father without the boy. Our father's life is bound up in the boy's life. [31] If he sees that the boy is not with us, our father will die. We, your servants, will indeed be responsible for sending that grieving, white-haired man to his grave. [32] My lord, I guaranteed to my father that I would take care of the boy. I told him, 'If I don't bring him back to you, I will bear the blame forever.' [33] So please, my lord, let me stay here as a slave instead of the boy, and let the boy return with his brothers. [34] For how can I return to my father if the boy is not with me? I couldn't bear to see the anguish this would cause my father!"

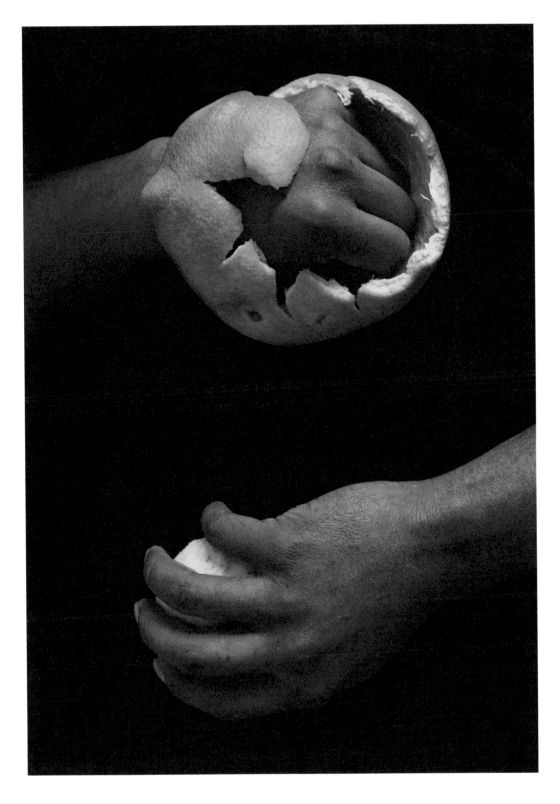

45

JOSEPH REVEALS HIS IDENTITY

[1] Joseph could stand it no longer. There were many people in the room, and he said to his attendants, "Out, all of you!" So he was alone with his brothers when he told them who he was. [2] Then he broke down and wept. He wept so loudly the Egyptians could hear him, and word of it quickly carried to Pharaoh's palace. [3] "I am Joseph!" he said to his brothers. "Is my father still alive?" But his brothers were speechless! They were stunned to realize that Joseph was standing there in front of them. [4] "Please, come closer," he said to them. So they came closer. And he said again, "I am Joseph, your brother, whom you sold into slavery in Egypt. [5] But don't be upset, and don't be angry with yourselves for selling me to this place. It was God who sent me here ahead of you to preserve your lives. [6] This famine that has ravaged the land for two years will last five more years, and there will be neither plowing nor harvesting. [7] God has sent me ahead of you to keep you and your families alive and to preserve many survivors. [8] So it was God who sent me here, not you! And he is the one who made me an adviser to Pharaoh—the manager of his entire palace and the governor of all Egypt. [9] Now hurry back to my father and tell him, 'This is what your son Joseph says: God has made me master over all the land of Egypt. So come down to me immediately! [10] You can live in the region of Goshen, where you can be near me with all your children and grandchildren, your flocks and herds, and everything you own. [11] I will take care of you there, for there are still five years of famine ahead of us. Otherwise you, your household, and all your animals will starve.'" [12] Then Joseph added, "Look! You can see for yourselves, and so can my brother Benjamin, that I really am Joseph! [13] Go tell my father of my honored position here in Egypt. Describe for him everything you have seen, and then bring my father here quickly." [14] Weeping with joy, he embraced Benjamin, and Benjamin did the same. [15] Then Joseph kissed each of his brothers and wept over them, and after that they began talking freely with him.

PHARAOH INVITES JACOB TO EGYPT

[16] The news soon reached Pharaoh's palace: "Joseph's brothers have arrived!" Pharaoh and his officials were all delighted to hear this. [17] Pharaoh said to Joseph, "Tell your brothers, 'This is what you must do: Load your pack animals, and hurry back to the land of Canaan. [18] Then get your father and all of your families, and return here to me. I will give you the very best land in Egypt, and you will eat from the best that the land produces.'" [19] Then Pharaoh said to Joseph, "Tell your brothers, 'Take wagons from the land of Egypt to carry your little children and your wives, and bring your father here. [20] Don't worry about your personal belongings, for the best of all the land of Egypt is yours.'" [21] So the sons of Jacob did as they were told. Joseph provided them with wagons, as Pharaoh had commanded, and he gave them supplies for the journey. [22] And he gave each of them new clothes—but to Benjamin he gave five changes of clothes and 300 pieces of silver. [23] He also sent his father ten male donkeys loaded with the finest products of Egypt, and ten female donkeys loaded with grain and bread and other supplies he would need on his journey. [24] So Joseph sent his brothers off, and as they left, he called after them, "Don't quarrel about all this along the way!" [25] And they left Egypt and returned to their father, Jacob, in the land of Canaan. [26] "Joseph is still alive!" they told him. "And he is governor of all the land of Egypt!" Jacob was stunned at the news—he couldn't believe it. [27] But when they repeated to Jacob everything Joseph had told them, and when he saw the wagons Joseph had sent to carry him, their father's spirits revived. [28] Then Jacob exclaimed, "It must be true! My son Joseph is alive! I must go and see him before I die."

46

JACOB'S JOURNEY TO EGYPT

¹ So Jacob set out for Egypt with all his possessions. And when he came to Beersheba, he offered sacrifices to the God of his father, Isaac. ² During the night God spoke to him in a vision. "Jacob! Jacob!" he called. "Here I am," Jacob replied. ³ "I am God, the God of your father," the voice said. "Do not be afraid to go down to Egypt, for there I will make your family into a great nation. ⁴ I will go with you down to Egypt, and I will bring you back again. You will die in Egypt, but Joseph will be with you to close your eyes." ⁵ So Jacob left Beersheba, and his sons took him to Egypt. They carried him and their little ones and their wives in the wagons Pharaoh had provided for them. ⁶ They also took all their livestock and all the personal belongings they had acquired in the land of Canaan. So Jacob and his entire family went to Egypt— ⁷ sons and grandsons, daughters and granddaughters— all his descendants. ⁸ These are the names of the descendants of Israel—the sons of Jacob—who went to Egypt: Reuben was Jacob's oldest son. ⁹ The sons of Reuben were Hanoch, Pallu, Hezron, and Carmi. ¹⁰ The sons of Simeon were Jemuel, Jamin, Ohad, Jakin, Zohar, and Shaul. (Shaul's mother was a Canaanite woman.) ¹¹ The sons of Levi were Gershon, Kohath, and Merari. ¹² The sons of Judah were Er, Onan, Shelah, Perez, and Zerah (though Er and Onan had died in the land of Canaan). The sons of Perez were Hezron and Hamul. ¹³ The sons of Issachar were Tola, Puah, Jashub, and Shimron. ¹⁴ The sons of Zebulun were Sered, Elon, and Jahleel. ¹⁵ These were the sons of Leah and Jacob who were born in Paddan-aram, in addition to their daughter, Dinah. The number of Jacob's descendants (male and female) through Leah was thirty-three. ¹⁶ The sons of Gad were Zephon, Haggi, Shuni, Ezbon, Eri, Arodi, and Areli. ¹⁷ The sons of Asher were Imnah, Ishvah, Ishvi, and Beriah. Their sister was Serah. Beriah's sons were Heber and Malkiel. ¹⁸ These were the sons of Zilpah, the servant given to Leah by her father, Laban. The number of Jacob's descendants through Zilpah was sixteen. ¹⁹ The sons of Jacob's wife Rachel were Joseph and Benjamin. ²⁰ Joseph's sons, born in the land of Egypt, were Manasseh and Ephraim. Their mother was Asenath, daughter of Potiphera, the priest of On. ²¹ Benjamin's sons were Bela, Beker, Ashbel, Gera, Naaman, Ehi, Rosh, Muppim, Huppim, and Ard. ²² These were the sons of Rachel and Jacob. The number of Jacob's descendants through Rachel was fourteen. ²³ The son of Dan was Hushim. ²⁴ The sons of Naphtali were Jahzeel, Guni, Jezer, and Shillem. ²⁵ These were the sons of Bilhah, the servant given to Rachel by her father, Laban. The number of Jacob's descendants through Bilhah was seven. ²⁶ The total number of Jacob's direct descendants who went with him to Egypt, not counting his sons' wives, was sixty-six. ²⁷ In addition, Joseph had two sons who were born in Egypt. So altogether, there were seventy members of Jacob's family in the land of Egypt.

JACOB'S FAMILY ARRIVES IN GOSHEN

[28] As they neared their destination, Jacob sent Judah ahead to meet Joseph and get directions to the region of Goshen. And when they finally arrived there, [29] Joseph prepared his chariot and traveled to Goshen to meet his father, Jacob. When Joseph arrived, he embraced his father and wept, holding him for a long time. [30] Finally, Jacob said to Joseph, "Now I am ready to die, since I have seen your face again and know you are still alive." [31] And Joseph said to his brothers and to his father's entire family, "I will go to Pharaoh and tell him, 'My brothers and my father's entire family have come to me from the land of Canaan. [32] These men are shepherds, and they raise livestock. They have brought with them their flocks and herds and everything they own.'" [33] Then he said, "When Pharaoh calls for you and asks you about your occupation, [34] you must tell him, 'We, your servants, have raised livestock all our lives, as our ancestors have always done.' When you tell him this, he will let you live here in the region of Goshen, for the Egyptians despise shepherds."

47

JACOB BLESSES PHARAOH

[1] Then Joseph went to see Pharaoh and told him, "My father and my brothers have arrived from the land of Canaan. They have come with all their flocks and herds and possessions, and they are now in the region of Goshen." [2] Joseph took five of his brothers with him and presented them to Pharaoh. [3] And Pharaoh asked the brothers, "What is your occupation?" They replied, "We, your servants, are shepherds, just like our ancestors. [4] We have come to live here in Egypt for a while, for there is no pasture for our flocks in Canaan. The famine is very severe there. So please, we request permission to live in the region of Goshen." [5] Then Pharaoh said to Joseph, "Now that your father and brothers have joined you here, [6] choose any place in the entire land of Egypt for them to live. Give them the best land of Egypt. Let them live in the region of Goshen. And if any of them have special skills, put them in charge of my livestock, too." [7] Then Joseph brought in his father, Jacob, and presented him to Pharaoh. And Jacob blessed Pharaoh. [8] "How old are you?" Pharaoh asked him. [9] Jacob replied, "I have traveled this earth for 130 hard years. But my life has been short compared to the lives of my ancestors." [10] Then Jacob blessed Pharaoh again before leaving his court. [11] So Joseph assigned the best land of Egypt—the region of Rameses—to his father and his brothers, and he settled them there, just as Pharaoh had commanded. [12] And Joseph provided food for his father and his brothers in amounts appropriate to the number of their dependents, including the smallest children.

JOSEPH'S LEADERSHIP IN THE FAMINE

[13] Meanwhile, the famine became so severe that all the food was used up, and people were starving throughout the lands of Egypt and Canaan. [14] By selling grain to the people, Joseph eventually collected all the money in Egypt and Canaan, and he put the money in Pharaoh's treasury. [15] When the people of Egypt and Canaan ran out of money, all the Egyptians came to Joseph. "Our money is gone!" they cried. "But please give us food, or we will die before your very eyes!" [16] Joseph replied, "Since your money is gone, bring me your livestock. I will give you food in exchange for your livestock." [17] So they brought their livestock to Joseph in exchange for food. In exchange for their horses, flocks of sheep and goats, herds of cattle, and donkeys, Joseph provided them with food for another year. [18] But that year ended, and the next year they came again and said, "We cannot hide the truth from you, my lord. Our money is gone, and all our livestock and cattle are yours. We have nothing left to give but our bodies and our land. [19] Why should we die before your very eyes? Buy us and our land in exchange for food; we offer our land and ourselves as slaves for Pharaoh. Just give us grain so we may live and not die, and so the land does not become empty and desolate." [20] So Joseph bought all the land of Egypt for Pharaoh. All the Egyptians sold him their fields because the famine was so severe, and soon all the land belonged to Pharaoh. [21] As for the people, he made them all slaves, from one end of Egypt to the other. [22] The only land he did not buy was the land belonging to the priests. They received an allotment of food directly from Pharaoh, so they didn't need to sell their land. [23] Then Joseph said to the people, "Look, today I have bought you and your land for Pharaoh. I will provide you with seed so you can plant the fields. [24] Then when you harvest it, one-fifth of your crop will belong to Pharaoh. You may keep the remaining four-fifths as seed for your fields and as food for you, your households, and your little ones." [25] "You have saved our lives!" they exclaimed. "May it please you, my lord, to let us be Pharaoh's servants." [26] Joseph then issued a decree still in effect in the land of Egypt, that Pharaoh should receive one-fifth of all the crops grown on his land. Only the land belonging to the priests was not given to Pharaoh. [27] Meanwhile, the people of Israel settled in the region of Goshen in Egypt. There they acquired property, and they were fruitful, and their population grew rapidly. [28] Jacob lived for seventeen years after his arrival in Egypt, so he lived 147 years in all. [29] As the time of his death drew near, Jacob called for his son Joseph and said to him, "Please do me this favor. Put your hand under my thigh and swear that you will treat me with unfailing love by honoring this last request: Do not bury me in Egypt. [30] When I die, please take my body out of Egypt and bury me with my ancestors." So Joseph promised, "I will do as you ask." [31] "Swear that you will do it," Jacob insisted. So Joseph gave his oath, and Jacob bowed humbly at the head of his bed.

48

JACOB BLESSES MANASSEH AND EPHRAIM

[1] One day not long after this, word came to Joseph, "Your father is failing rapidly." So Joseph went to visit his father, and he took with him his two sons, Manasseh and Ephraim. [2] When Joseph arrived, Jacob was told, "Your son Joseph has come to see you." So Jacob gathered his strength and sat up in his bed. [3] Jacob said to Joseph, "God Almighty appeared to me at Luz in the land of Canaan and blessed me. [4] He said to me, 'I will make you fruitful, and I will multiply your descendants. I will make you a multitude of nations. And I will give this land of Canaan to your descendants after you as an everlasting possession.' [5] Now I am claiming as my own sons these two boys of yours, Ephraim and Manasseh, who were born here in the land of Egypt before I arrived. They will be my sons, just as Reuben and Simeon are. [6] But any children born to you in the future will be your own, and they will inherit land within the territories of their brothers Ephraim and Manasseh. [7] Long ago, as I was returning from Paddan-aram, Rachel died in the land of Canaan. We were still on the way, some distance from Ephrath (that is, Bethlehem). So with great sorrow I buried her there beside the road to Ephrath." [8] Then Jacob looked over at the two boys. "Are these your sons?" he asked. [9] "Yes," Joseph told him, "these are the sons God has given me here in Egypt." And Jacob said, "Bring them closer to me, so I can bless them." [10] Jacob was half blind because of his age and could hardly see. So Joseph brought the boys close to him, and Jacob kissed and embraced them. [11] Then Jacob said to Joseph, "I never thought I would see your face again, but now God has let me see your children, too!" [12] Joseph moved the boys, who were at their grandfather's knees, and he bowed with his face to the ground. [13] Then he positioned the boys in front of Jacob. With his right hand he directed Ephraim toward Jacob's left hand, and with his left hand he put Manasseh at Jacob's right hand. [14] But Jacob crossed his arms as he reached out to lay his hands on the boys' heads. He put his right hand on the head of Ephraim, though he was the younger boy, and his left hand on the head of Manasseh, though he was the firstborn. [15] Then he blessed Joseph and said, "May the God before whom my grandfather Abraham and my father, Isaac, walked— the God who has been my shepherd all my life, to this very day, [16] the Angel who has redeemed me from all harm—may he bless these boys. May they preserve my name and the names of Abraham and Isaac. And may their descendants multiply greatly throughout the earth." [17] But Joseph was upset when he saw that his father placed his right hand on Ephraim's head. So Joseph lifted it to move it from Ephraim's head to Manasseh's head. [18] "No, my father," he said. "This one is the firstborn. Put your right hand on his head." [19] But his father refused. "I know, my son; I know," he replied. "Manasseh will also become a great people, but his younger brother will become even greater. And his descendants will become a multitude of nations." [20] So Jacob blessed the boys that day with this blessing: "The people of Israel will use your names when they give a blessing. They will say, 'May God make you as prosperous as Ephraim and Manasseh.'" In this way, Jacob put Ephraim ahead of Manasseh. [21] Then Jacob said to Joseph, "Look, I am about to die, but God will be with you and will take you back to Canaan, the land of your ancestors. [22] And beyond what I have given your brothers, I am giving you an extra portion of the land that I took from the Amorites with my sword and bow."

49

JACOB'S LAST WORDS TO HIS SONS

¹ Then Jacob called together all his sons and said, "Gather around me, and I will tell you what will happen to each of you in the days to come. ² Come and listen, you sons of Jacob; listen to Israel, your father. ³ Reuben, you are my firstborn, my strength, the child of my vigorous youth. You are first in rank and first in power. ⁴ But you are as unruly as a flood, and you will be first no longer. For you went to bed with my wife; you defiled my marriage couch. ⁵ Simeon and Levi are two of a kind; their weapons are instruments of violence. ⁶ May I never join in their meetings; may I never be a party to their plans. For in their anger they murdered men, and they crippled oxen just for sport. ⁷ A curse on their anger, for it is fierce; a curse on their wrath, for it is cruel. I will scatter them among the descendants of Jacob; I will disperse them throughout Israel. ⁸ Judah, your brothers will praise you. You will grasp your enemies by the neck. All your relatives will bow before you. ⁹ Judah, my son, is a young lion that has finished eating its prey. Like a lion he crouches and lies down; like a lioness— who dares to rouse him? ¹⁰ The scepter will not depart from Judah, nor the ruler's staff from his descendants, until the coming of the one to whom it belongs, the one whom all nations will honor. ¹¹

He ties his foal to a grapevine, the colt of his donkey to a choice vine. He washes his clothes in wine, his robes in the blood of grapes. ¹² His eyes are darker than wine, and his teeth are whiter than milk. ¹³ Zebulun will settle by the seashore and will be a harbor for ships; his borders will extend to Sidon. ¹⁴ Issachar is a sturdy donkey, resting between two saddlepacks. ¹⁵ When he sees how good the countryside is and how pleasant the land, he will bend his shoulder to the load and submit himself to hard labor. ¹⁶ Dan will govern his people, like any other tribe in Israel. ¹⁷ Dan will be a snake beside the road, a poisonous viper along the path that bites the horse's hooves so its rider is thrown off. ¹⁸ I trust in you for salvation, O Lord! ¹⁹ Gad will be attacked by marauding bands, but he will attack them when they retreat. ²⁰ Asher will dine on rich foods and produce food fit for kings. ²¹ Naphtali is a doe set free that bears beautiful fawns. ²² Joseph is the foal of a wild donkey, the foal of a wild donkey at a spring—one of the wild donkeys on the ridge. ²³ Archers attacked him savagely; they shot at him and harassed him. ²⁴ But his bow remained taut, and his arms were strengthened by the hands of the Mighty One of Jacob, by the Shepherd, the Rock of Israel. ²⁵ May the God of your father help you; may the Almighty bless you with the blessings of the heavens above, and blessings of the watery depths below, and blessings of the breasts and womb. [26] May my fatherly blessings on you surpass the blessings of my ancestors, reaching to the heights of the eternal hills. May these blessings rest on the head of Joseph, who is a prince among his brothers. [27] Benjamin is a ravenous wolf, devouring his enemies in the morning and dividing his plunder in the evening." [28] These are the twelve tribes of Israel, and this is what their father said as he told his sons good-bye. He blessed each one with an appropriate message.

JACOB'S DEATH AND BURIAL

[29] Then Jacob instructed them, "Soon I will die and join my ancestors. Bury me with my father and grandfather in the cave in the field of Ephron the Hittite. [30] This is the cave in the field of Machpelah, near Mamre in Canaan, that Abraham bought from Ephron the Hittite as a permanent burial site. [31] There Abraham and his wife Sarah are buried. There Isaac and his wife, Rebekah, are buried. And there I buried Leah. [32] It is the plot of land and the cave that my grandfather Abraham bought from the Hittites." [33] When Jacob had finished this charge to his sons, he drew his feet into the bed, breathed his last, and joined his ancestors in death.

50

¹ Joseph threw himself on his father and wept over him and kissed him. ² Then Joseph told the physicians who served him to embalm his father's body; so Jacob was embalmed. ³ The embalming process took the usual forty days. And the Egyptians mourned his death for seventy days. ⁴ When the period of mourning was over, Joseph approached Pharaoh's advisers and said, "Please do me this favor and speak to Pharaoh on my behalf. ⁵ Tell him that my father made me swear an oath. He said to me, 'Listen, I am about to die. Take my body back to the land of Canaan, and bury me in the tomb I prepared for myself.' So please allow me to go and bury my father. After his burial, I will return without delay." ⁶ Pharaoh agreed to Joseph's request. "Go and bury your father, as he made you promise," he said. ⁷ So Joseph went up to bury his father. He was accompanied by all of Pharaoh's officials, all the senior members of Pharaoh's household, and all the senior officers of Egypt. ⁸ Joseph also took his entire household and his brothers and their households. But they left their little children and flocks and herds in the land of Goshen. ⁹ A great number of chariots and charioteers accompanied Joseph. ¹⁰ When they arrived at the threshing floor of Atad, near the Jordan River, they held a very great and solemn memorial service, with a seven-day period of mourning for Joseph's father. ¹¹ The local residents, the Canaanites, watched them mourning at the threshing floor of Atad. Then they renamed that place (which is near the Jordan) Abel-mizraim, for they said, "This is a place of deep mourning for these Egyptians." ¹² So Jacob's sons did as he had commanded them. ¹³ They carried his body to the land of Canaan and buried him in the cave in the field of Machpelah, near Mamre. This is the cave that Abraham had bought as a permanent burial site from Ephron the Hittite.

JOSEPH REASSURES HIS BROTHERS

[14] After burying Jacob, Joseph returned to Egypt with his brothers and all who had accompanied him to his father's burial. [15] But now that their father was dead, Joseph's brothers became fearful. "Now Joseph will show his anger and pay us back for all the wrong we did to him," they said. [16] So they sent this message to Joseph: "Before your father died, he instructed us [17] to say to you: 'Please forgive your brothers for the great wrong they did to you—for their sin in treating you so cruelly.' So we, the servants of the God of your father, beg you to forgive our sin." When Joseph received the message, he broke down and wept. [18] Then his brothers came and threw themselves down before Joseph. "Look, we are your slaves!" they said. [19] But Joseph replied, "Don't be afraid of me. Am I God, that I can punish you? [20] You intended to harm me, but God intended it all for good. He brought me to this position so I could save the lives of many people. [21] No, don't be afraid. I will continue to take care of you and your children." So he reassured them by speaking kindly to them.

THE DEATH OF JOSEPH

[22] So Joseph and his brothers and their families continued to live in Egypt. Joseph lived to the age of 110. [23] He lived to see three generations of descendants of his son Ephraim, and he lived to see the birth of the children of Manasseh's son Makir, whom he claimed as his own. [24] "Soon I will die," Joseph told his brothers, "but God will surely come to help you and lead you out of this land of Egypt. He will bring you back to the land he solemnly promised to give to Abraham, to Isaac, and to Jacob." [25] Then Joseph made the sons of Israel swear an oath, and he said, "When God comes to help you and lead you back, you must take my bones with you." [26] So Joseph died at the age of 110. The Egyptians embalmed him, and his body was placed in a coffin in Egypt.

♦ ALABASTER

CO-FOUNDER, MANAGING DIRECTOR
Brian Chung

CO-FOUNDER, CREATIVE DIRECTOR
Bryan Ye-Chung

OPERATIONS DIRECTOR
Willa Jin

STUDIO MANAGER
Tyler Zak

CONTENT EDITOR
Darin McKenna

COVER IMAGE
Bryan Ye-Chung

STUDIO AND SUPPORT ASSISTANTS
Abigail Leung
Jared Yamasaki
Justin Lee
Kay Xie

SPECIAL THANKS
Josephine Law, Original Designer

ALABASTER

PHOTOGRAPHERS

Abigail Leung
Bryan Ye-Chung
Carmen Leung
Echo Chen
Evan Rummel
Heidi Parra
Ian Teraoka
Jacob Chung
Jonathan Martin
Kristen Hahn
Lois Lee
Luke McNeal
Makito Umekita
Michelle S. Palafox
Salomé Watel
Samuel Park
Tyler Zak

ARTISTS

Bryan Ye-Chung
Oil on Canvas, 2019

MODELS

Abigail Rugg
Alan Zeng
Alex Wada
Alexander Mossman
Arrah Enaw
Daniel Sunkari
Giovanny Panginda
Ian Teraoka
Isabel Vaguirre
Jared Yamasaki
Jon Webster
Justin Lee
Kealani
Kamakeeaina
Kiersten Asbill Chow
Matthew Harris
Moses Holley
Stefanie Rouse
Steve Macario
Taryn Cheng

CONTINUE THE CONVERSATION
www.alabasterco.com